WINNERS

WINNERS

by

Robert Bruce

SIDGWICK & JACKSON

LONDON

First published in Great Britain in 1986
by Sidgwick & Jackson Limited

Copyright © Robert Bruce 1986

ISBN   0-283-99416-9

Phototypeset by Action Typesetting,
Assurance House, 1 Russell Street, Gloucester
Printed in Great Britain by Martin's of Berwick,
Spittal, Berwick upon Tweed and
Bound in Great Britain by Hunter & Foulis,
McDonald Road, Edinburgh
for Sidgwick & Jackson Limited
1 Tavistock Chambers, Bloomsbury Way,
London WC1A 2SG

For my parents

CONTENTS

This book would not have been possible without the help of many people. First and most obviously the "Winners" themselves. Without exception they have been both helpful and hospitable, usually at times when it was obvious they would much rather be out there running their businesses than sitting down and just talking about them.

Secondly we all owe a great debt of gratitude to what is now the corporate finance division of Lloyds Bowmaker. It is their continued backing of the award which has enabled the winners to gain the recognition they deserved. Peter Hook, director of the corporate finance division, in particular has provided an immense amount of support. In the early days, Gordon Walters, and latterly, John Allsopp, have done a tremendous job in unobtrusively and meticulously administering the award.

The annual judging of the award has been both thoroughly efficient and greatly enjoyable. This is very largely due to the extraordinary skills of the chairman of the panel, Sir Monty Finniston. His remarkable abilities have made a great contribution to the award's success.

I would also like to thank the judges over the years for their wisdom, arguments and ability to arrive, eventually, at a happy agreement. Gerry Bradshaw, Brandon Gough, Robert Smith, Alan Stote, Jeremy Pope and Denis Fredjohn have all been excellent companions round the judging table.

All of these winners were first written about in the pages of *Accountancy Age*, that great reflector of all that is important in the accountancy world. I would like to thank Ian Griffiths, Nigel Tutt and Jane Simms who wrote the initial articles on three of the winners.

A special thanks goes to Barbara Jones whose diligent efforts at making sense of the taped conversations which contributed so much to this book, were remarkable.

I would also like to thank Simon Cook and John Leslie, publishing director and publisher, respectively, of *Accountancy Age*, for allowing me as editor of that newspaper the time to write this book. Thanks also go to all my colleagues on the paper who have run it so admirably during my erratic absences.

And finally, Sarah. I am, she tells me, an awkward soul at the best of times. But the completion of this book is in many ways due to her patience and inspiration. All my thanks go finally to her.

INTRODUCTION

We have the reputation as a nation of being good losers. This means that when we lose we do not cry "We wuz robbed". or bemoan the unfairness of the Goddess Luck or decry the merits of the winners; but the fact remains that this generosity of spirit only dissembles the truth, namely that winning is to be preferred to losing. This book is about five groups of people who did make the grade.

I have had the good fortune and exciting experience of being the Chairman of the judges who have had to choose a winner from the many entrants for the Industrial Achievement Award. But picking winners, as everybody knows, is not easy. In this case the task demanded a concentration of effort in the greatest detail to determine the final discriminating choice between the six or so on the short list. All the factual information provided by the entrants — financial, commercial, administrative etc — has to be analysed; a critical view of the weaknesses as well as strength of the balance sheet and profit and loss account has to be taken; market judgements based on the past and projected into the future have to be discounted (rarely otherwise) for optimism; the merits and demerits of the product design in relation to the competition have to be considered; assessment of

1

management strength and their commitment to the company has to be made; comparison with other entrants etc etc etc.

These considerations which assess future potential success or otherwise of the product or process cannot be simply determined by ticking various features on some arbitrary numerical scale. What was remarkable was how the views of all the judges arrived at independently, even though debated at length, came to the same conclusions unanimously.

This book is a record of the winners themselves. Everybody agrees on the value to the economy of creating small businesses. But what lessons are to be learned from the successes of the reported five? At least the following factors are essential ingredients: character and hard work. Character means courage and commitment, and only in the dictionary does success come before work; and neither is confined to the male sex.

We as a nation are not just good losers. We do produce good winners; even the runners up are winners in the industrial world though they did not quite manage first place in the Awards. If the judges have any regrets, it is that we could not make a wider distribution of the awards to those who entered the competition. But they, too, deserve praise — in another book.

Monty Finniston
May 1986

INTRODUCTION

This book sets out to explain a simple and straight-forward idea which is often made to seem complex and discouraging.

The idea is that of starting a business and building it into a substantial enterprise.

For many people the achievement of such a task seems impossibly remote. It is not even something that they would think about in their idle moments. For a few people it is an achievement which has transformed their lives.

In this book I have tried to tell the story, from initial idea to present-day reality, of five winners in the business world. The important point behind these five is that they were all started by ordinary and straightforward people. They are still, to a greater or lesser extent, run by them.

None of them were started by a team of business experts who decided to use their skills in the financial world to run a business which would give them the power and the money which are traditionally seen to be the aim of bright young accountants, or business graduates, in the City or in industry.

The five case studies are those of the first five winners of the annual Industrial Achievement award. This award, which is sponsored by Lloyds Bowmaker and *Accountancy Age*, aims to recognise new ideas, products, processes or markets.

The intention has always been to look for companies which had been created to fill a gap in the market, or which had transformed themselves through the implementation of a new product or idea into a totally different company.

Over the last five years it has found them in abundance.

In the award's first year, when it was sponsored by Bowmakers, Development Capital and *Accountancy* magazine, the winners were Rita and Bert Battersby, who had founded VDU Installations.

These two realised that in a computer world where electrical experts and computer experts knew much about their own worlds, but little about each others', there was a need for someone to provide all the specialised cabling services to connect the two.

The whole business started on the dining room table with personal letters being written off to potential customers. By 1985 turnover was over £2 million with over 100 employees.

In 1982, when *Accountancy Age* joined Bowmakers as sponsors, the winners were Microvitec. This was the brainchild of Tony Martinez, who had come to this country from Spain as a teenager and spent his career in the electronics industry. He saw there was need for a cheap, but sturdy, colour monitor for use with computerised systems, whether they are for businesses, schools or Space Invaders games.

His company has since made a spectacular debut on the Unlisted Securities Market as well as suffering all the triumphs and disasters of that risky sector. Turnover in 1985 was £29.75 million with 350 employees.

In 1983 the winners were Norfrost, a company started by Pat and Alec Grant a stone's throw from John O'Groats in the far north of Scotland.

They built their first freezer in their spare bedroom, and now turn out 3,000 a week. Turnover in 1986 was just under £6 million with over 120 employees.

In 1984 the award went to Denford Machine Tools, a family-run business in Brighouse, Yorkshire. Once a fading

4

company in the declining machine-tool sector, it was transformed by one new idea and product range, pioneered with determination by Gerald Denford and his team. Turnover in 1986 was just over £5 million with 125 employees.

Finally in 1985 the award went to Industrial Cleaning Services run by Gio Benedetti in Ayrshire. He had arrived on the west coast of Scotland as a small boy, who spoke no English, to work in an uncle's cafe. Determination and an eye for opportunities has meant he has created a company which, through the development of an industrial glove cleaning process saving the British car industry alone several millions of pounds a year, has grown spectacularly. Turnover in 1986 was £2.8 million with 215 employees.

Those are the five winners. There is no reason why many more people could not emulate their success. None of them had any financial or particular business acumen before they set up their businesses. None of them had been to university or to business school. Their example explodes the myth that successful business people are born with a knowledge of VAT systems, tax dodges or corporate strategy already embedded in their busily calculating minds.

All of these people are ordinary people. The only thing that has made them extraordinary is that they have put an idea into practice and by the simple application of hard work and common sense, mixed with a large amount of determination, have become winners.

I have tried to tell their stories in a simple way. I have allowed them to speak with their own voices. There has been no attempt to make it into a sophisticated piece of business jargon for bright young pinstripes to spar with in conversation. Moreover I have tried not to write it in the style of a 'business' or 'management' book. Such books are usually written to bolster the egos of erstwhile management gurus and boost the veneer of their acolytes in business. All they do is alternately create and destroy the recurring myths which make the understanding of business so remote a concept to most people.

This book is about ordinary people who have become business winners. All that they have done, and the way that they have done it, is set down in an attempt to show that most management and business skills derive from common-sense and enthusiasm.

My hope is that people reading this book may come to realise there is no great barrier which prevents people from being successful in business and that it is not a stressful desk-bound grind.

All these winners have worked long hours and have battled against the prospect of defeat. In turn they have all derived an immense amount of fun and satisfaction from the experience.

FIRST WINNER:
VDU INSTALLATIONS

VDU Installations was the first winner of the Industrial Achievement award back in 1981. Right from the beginning the pattern of success was set.

The company was essentially a husband-and-wife team and, like Norfrost, which won the award in 1983, it was the wife who provided the essential drive and feel for business decisions while the husband supplied the relevant technical knowledge.

They had noticed a gap in the market, and began the company partly out of irritation that a sophisticated sector of industry had simply not thought hard enough about the needs of its customers. With very little previous business experience when they set up, most decisions were necessarily based on a combination of common sense and their own hunches.

They set about the task of running their business with enthusiasm and plenty of hard work and long hours. In common with other winners of the award they still, despite having achieved their success, work hard and long at the business. They thoroughly enjoy it.

Theirs is a story of how a couple of determined people with a good idea and a belief that they could win actually managed it.

1

Bert and Rita Battersby come from very similar backgrounds. They were both born in the same ward of a maternity hospital near Preston, Lancashire, although three years apart. They first met when Rita was 14 and Bert 17. She was his first steady girlfriend and they married seven years later.

Bert trained as a Post Office engineer when he left school, then spent his National Service with the Royal Signals, before rejoining the Post Office in Staffordshire, then returned to Preston and worked for the Electricity Board. Tellingly, a personnel report on him there reveals that he was "intolerant of lazy people".

In 1969 Bert joined IBM as a field engineer and worked out of Richmond in an area support group looking after Africa, Scandinavia and parts of the UK. It was there he became a specialist engineer responsible for new product installations.

Meanwhile Rita was helping a friend to set up an employment agency. Between them they were unwittingly acquiring the relevant experience and confidence which in time to come would enable them to run their own business. It would not be an obstacle at which they would hesitate and then not pursue.

Bert had learned all about cables at the Post Office and Electricity Board and all about computers at IBM. He had also learned one other thing from working in the two industries: "There were two industries here which simply didn't talk to each other". That annoyed him.

By the mid-seventies, the computer world had an abundance of experts to advise people on what sort of computer to use and what peripheral equipment to buy to complement it. Equally there was no shortage of electrical contractors who would sort out the power points.

Yet there was a major flaw of which Bert was aware. The users of these new computers had no idea of what sort of cables and connectors were needed to link their new systems together so that visual display units, printers and computers could all do what the buyer wanted. Moreover, the electrical contractors had very little idea of what computers were all about.

Bert believed a specialist company was required which could provide advice, supply and, if necessary, install all the cables and connectors needed to link properly the various elements of the system. Bert and Rita Battersby set up VDU Installations Limited to fill the niche.

2

Due to a career move by Bert with IBM the Battersbys moved house and Rita's work with the employment agency ended. She decided that having helped set up a business once she would like to do it again.

"Initially I was going to open another employment agency because I knew how to do that. I didn't really want to get involved in setting up a company dealing with cables and connectors because I didn't know anything about computers", she says.

"Bert said 'that doesn't matter, I'll show you how'." VDUI was founded in 1977 with £100 of share capital.

With the pressure of a mortgage they decided the business would have to be run in the evenings. Rita would stay at her local job during the day and Bert would stay with IBM.

To begin with the plan was simply to write to potential customers offering their service. Rita looked through job advertisements for programmers and, on the assumption that any operation expanding their computer installations with new staff would also be in need of VDUI's new services, wrote to the managers recruiting new staff.

"We thought we would stand more chance of someone reading our letters if they were individually typed rather than copies. It also cost less money. So every evening I would sit down and type the letters. I probably wrote over 1,000 letters on my manual typewriter", comments Rita.

Avoiding the 'standard letter' approach paid off. In any case they couldn't have afforded anything more sophisticated. Bert points out: "70% of my mail every morning is just mail shot stuff, and gets binned". The approach worked both initially and long-term. One of the first letters that Rita sent out was put on file by a potential customer. "They ordered for the first time a year later and have been ordering once a month ever since", says Bert.

At this stage they had another partner who had become

9

interested in Bert's ideas and had agreed to put up some money. The promises came to nothing, but for the first year the partner's drawings of petty cash was the only money being taken out of the company. "Rita put in all the hard work", Bert explains, "but the promised capital never came in. In fact Rita worked for a complete year without drawing anything out of the business".

Rita takes up the story: "We effectively hadn't got any working capital. We could have gone to the bank and said, 'well, here's our house as security' but we had worked very hard to get the house and didn't want to gamble with it."

"We installed an answering machine. I'd also come home in my lunch break and take some of the calls". At that time Rita was working 8 until 4 at her other job, "so I'd have two hours when I got home to call them back".

"The calls started to flow in. I always had a long question and answer sheet by me which Bert and I had worked out on the basis of 'what do I say if they ask this?' and 'what if they ask that?' Bert was very helpful and kept telling me that, in most cases, I would probably know more about it than they would."

With hindsight the Battersbys realise they were operating a classical marketing exercise in which they did little other than emphasise the benefits of their proposed services.

Rita continues: "With Bert translating the technical side and identifying customer requirements, all I was selling were the benefits. They loved it. If they went to any other company and asked for particular requirements, they were getting through to accountants or managing directors who didn't know much about computers. Whereas when they got through to me, they were talking to someone who didn't have a computer background but who had made the effort to understand them from a layman's point of view."

"I knew the essentials. You just need to know 'Here's a computer, I want it talking to this one and talking to that one and I want you to do it'. I would say 'fine, which system have you got?' There wasn't even the need to worry about particular types of cable because Bert had already sorted out a list of which needed what."

Like most good business ideas it sounds so startlingly simple now, one wonders why it wasn't obvious to the rest of the industry at the time. "We did have competitors at the time because electrical contractors could do what we were doing. What they didn't have was any experience of the computer industry. Neither did I. But Bert did."

Bert explains: "We won because of the simplicity of our approach combined with our ability to give the customer confidence that it would all work. Unlike our competitors we never gave our customers long drawn out specifications when we knew they wouldn't understand a word of them. Rita's sales voice and the personal letter convinced them."

They were still having problems raising the promised capital from their prospective partner but enough cash was coming in and the volume of work increasing. The plan had been to grow slowly but steadily. They were doing that and meanwhile establishing a solid base of good customers. Their first ever order came from the British Sugar Corporation, for example. It was time for Rita to give up her day job and to open their first office.

"At a rent of £9 a week we opened an eight foot by six foot office with little bars over the windows in Camberley," notes Bert. "Rita, myself and our daughters painted it over a weekend. It was terribly wet and damp. We covered the damp patches with wood panelling and put a telephone in."

"That phone never stopped ringing", adds Rita. Sales which had averaged £5,000 a month doubled. For the year to 31 August 1979, sales reached £115,000 and pre-tax profits hit £21,000. "I've always done the accounts side", she says. "But in those days I had to do all the books at home in the evening because there wasn't time during the day. If there was an urgent call for cable then I'd have to nip out of the office, lift a 32 kilo drum of cable into the boot of the car and try to get the Escort out onto the London Road, which was difficult as it's a very busy road."

"Then I'd get down to the British Rail Red Star parcels office. I'm not very tall but they'd never give me a hand.

They'd just stand there watching me lift it out of the boot and lug it into the office''.

The upsurge in activity brought financing problems. Bert recalls "the biggest problem was that we had no capital. Rita had to convince customers, even the largest companies, to pay us before they got the goods".

"I don't know how we had the cheek to do it", says Rita, "but we managed to sell it as a service. They would pay me and I would go out and get the goods from somewhere. To buy ten connectors I might have to go to ten suppliers because at that time we had no track record".

The financing problems put a strain on their relationship with their partner. The capital he had promised had failed to materialise and he was drawing more out of the company in expenses than Rita's salary, the heat, light and office rent put together.

"We decided he had to go", says Bert. "It cost us nearly two years' profits to buy him out and took nearly all our working capital. We had to start all over again." At the same time they decided to go for larger premises, and managed to find an old Victorian house in Windlesham which had been a jeweller's shop. Rita went to the bank to borrow money for the first time. The new premises were going to cost £60,000. Barclays came up with £40,000, the rest came from cash flow. They ran the office upstairs and opened the ground floor as a lighting shop in what would later prove a vain attempt to avoid the need for planning permission for their offices.

The company was now growing at such a rate that the Battersbys decided Bert should give up his job with IBM and join VDUI full time. Bert left IBM in November 1979 and his added help paid off. Turnover, which had averaged £9,000 a month before he joined, averaged nearly £30,000 a month over the remaining nine months of the year to 31 August 1980.

They solved the problem of a husband-and-wife team by becoming joint managing directors, though Rita's original thoughts had been different. "Just because I'm a woman I'd thought 'my goodness, here's Bert giving up his good career because I've gone out and got this company going'. I said 'well, you'll have to be managing director'.'' The joint arrangement suits them. Rita runs and directs the company and Bert provides the technical expertise for both customers and the growing numbers of engineers and staff. The problems come from outside. ''At work the marriage stops'', Rita points out. ''In here we're just people in meetings.'' But the attitudes of some people irritate her.

''I don't like the idea of big-headed and bolshie businesswomen,'' she says, ''but the outside world has made it very difficult at times. When we won the Industrial Achievement award people would say things to me like, 'you're the tax fiddle are you?' or 'you're his secretary then?'. I realised that because I was a woman it was automatically assumed I had nothing to do with the success. That hurt a bit, because although I felt I didn't need to be recognised by the outside world, I also felt if the outside world was going to take a look at us it should recognise what I'd done.''

''It didn't affect Bert and I at all. He felt upset by it as well''. Then when an OBE came along it went to Bert rather than Rita ''presumably for the same reasons, as it said it was for the business. I knew he was going to get it before he did. I took the phone call from the Ministry when they asked all about his background and went through the preliminaries. If they'd just given it to him for being such a super guy then I would have understood. But I was the one who had built the business.'' In turn Bert gets fed up with finding that much of the post is sent automatically to the joint managing director called Bert rather than to the joint managing director called Rita. ''It makes you into a feminist'', he smiles.

3

They won the Industrial Achievement award in 1981. ''We entered it because we needed the money and there were no strings attached to the £10,000 prize. It was a super time and we can't thank Bowmaker enough. They provided an incentive in the same way that the Government keeps saying it will but never does. They took a look at us and said 'you're doing really well and deserve a reward, recognition for your achievements' ", Bert says gratefully.

After that: "We were offered money for the company and hundreds of financial advisors sprang up all over the place, but Rita stuck to her basic principle of putting what we made back into the company."

"VDUI continued to grow and we started taking on our first employees. We began to get export enquiries by telephone, we got a better name in the industry by word of mouth, we took on more people, we moved to Windlesham, organised stores premises in Chobham and then took a temporary lease on a building in Brookwoods".

At this point they were involved in a number of decisions which, in theory, should have eased their growth. In fact they ate up management time in bitter wrangles with the local authorities.

The first of these was the battle over planning permission to allow the use of the Windlesham premises for business purposes. This lasted for the whole of their time there, and together with other arguments, left the Battersbys disillusioned with the way in which small companies are treated by local authorities.

Bert and Rita bought the place, which consisted of a house, workshop and ground floor shop, on the basis that if it is cheaper to buy with a mortgage than to rent, then premises should be bought. The idea of buying an asset as part of expanding the business has obvious attractions to the common sense approach.

There was only one snag. The Battersbys did not have the relevant permission to operate a computer company from the Windlesham property, which were technically private premises. An initial approach to the local council suggested that little objection would be made if they went ahead with their plans. However, in an effort at appeasement, the Battersbys reopened the shop at the front selling and repairing electrical goods. Called Microlec, it wasn't a huge success, but the strategy was never to make a fortune out of it.

Rita recalls: "We then applied for planning permission because it did have a small workshop where the previous owner

14

used to repair watches. That was turned down at first, but then it got through. So we had planning permission downstairs. The next challenge was to get it upstairs''. They had a further incentive here. "Our accountant had told us that if we got permission for the upstairs then it would become a real asset because of the shortage of office space in the village."

Then they got involved with a car park. They provided a small one behind the shop and tried to make a case that the village could use it in return for their gaining planning permission for the upstairs offices. The result was chaos. The people opposite accused them of creating parking problems in the village. Meanwhile a petition supporting VDUI's efforts to stay in the village, and have their car park, went round the houses.

The petition was turned down. However, following a further wrangle with the authorities, "we got a letter saying that we'd got upstairs permission," sighs Rita. By that time they were expanding out of the premises anyway, but it meant that they could keep the banks happy by putting a now valuable office building into their company pension fund while renting it out to a firm of estate agents, bringing in further revenue.

The Battersbys' final wrangle with the local authorities concerned their pension fund.

Bert explains: "I made a silly mistake under pressure over a decision regarding putting money into pension funds. The funny thing was that we'd set up a company pension fund, but because I was the only one with a break in service, Rita and I were without a pension. All the other employees had them. I decided to buy some land in Chobham and made the mistake of thinking that it could eventually go into a pension fund."

"At the time the Government had just issued a statement saying that derelict farm buildings were to be used for light industry. Prince Charles was doing his rounds of the country saying what a good job people were making of creating small businesses in workshop units."

"We bought some land from a company which had previously employed 70 people growing trees. They'd been made redundant and all that was left was the land and the derelict buildings."

15

The idea was for the pension fund to own the land and new buildings they would build. As they outgrew Windlesham they would move into their own new purpose-built workshops and offices. Moreover, they would retain their principle of owning the building in which they worked.

The problem was that in Green Belt land the rules do not get bent for small businesses. Their efforts to get planning permission were rejected. Bert and Rita are bitter, not just about that particular decision, but about the whole area of incentives. The patch of land remains a problem to the council. It is hardly beautiful with 22,000 square feet of derelict buildings on it, yet technically it cannot be redeveloped.

"Even though we were living in Surrey, the strongest Conservative area in the country, I am afraid that whatever Maggie Thatcher is saying about providing incentives to small businesses, it doesn't get through to local level. The buildings are still derelict and the whole affair has cost us a lot of money."

In Bert's opinion: "Local authorities in Conservative areas are run by colonels who have always had everything guaranteed for them in life. They've never actually had to make a living."

Although they got into the arguments by mistake, the Battersbys see the issues as wider than that of simple land-use: "The biggest stumbling-block for small businesses", says Rita, "is becoming larger businesses. There aren't many who have made that step. It's partly because you have to be so determined and committed."

"There's no real incentive for the small businessman to do it because you can earn as much money often by being small. We have to stay near London and the City because that's where our customers are. So there is no incentive to us in knowing that you can get a grant or a deal if you move to Wales or Scotland. Our customers dictate where we have to be."

"The stumbling-block for all small business people is that unless they are prepared to grow they are forced into a position of accepting they will probably lose their market, or they've got to take this horrendous step and accept all the disadvantages that come from moving up in scale. There isn't any real incentive to do it.''

The affair of the factory 'that never was' changed their attitudes. As far as Rita is concerned the green-belt argument was a nonsense given the state of the land they had bought.

''It would make basic common-sense that if one industry dies and another one can take its place, and not cause any damage to the environment, it should be allowed to do so. That seems common-sense to us. After they had rejected our plans we rather lost faith in what people were saying about encouraging small business. We realised that if you are in business then you're on your own. You either take that decision to go forward and grow with the business, create new jobs and accept all the responsibilities that go with it. Or you sell out to someone else, totally forget about it all, and go off to the South of France.''

''If you're not that kind of person and you like this country then you've got to go through with it.''

The whole episode also reinforced their belief in sticking to your talents. Bert sums it up: ''Our strength is running the business and not dealing with local authorities or worrying about what happens if we both cop it in a car crash.''

Ironically, when their appeal to re-develop the land was finally turned down, the permission to use the Windlesham premises as offices came through. It was useful but the time had passed for offices of that size.

4

VDUI is now settled, discreetly but solidly, on a new and very impressive estate in Bracknell. They are opposite British Aerospace and the then minister for small business, David Trippier, opened the building in October 1985. It has all the hallmarks of the successful hi-tech company headquarters. Above all it exudes confidence. Bert Battersby predictably takes another view: ''The lavatories all blocked up on the second day'', he says. Another trial for the small businessman.

The new building has 20,000 square feet of space. The front area houses the offices and the back is a clean and clear warehouse and testing area. The approach is still one of a small customer-led operation. In the warehouse you will find shelves with odd short lengths of cable on them. "That", as Bert explains, "is our 'no scrap' policy. Any cable we don't use on a particular job we bring back, even if it's as short as two metres. Then if they move a desk and need some more custom-built cabling, we've got it here, and we can install it there, fast." The company's slogan is now 'Be Well Connected'.

They have also established a small 5,000 square foot factory which allows them to manufacture some of their supplies. The strong Northern influence apparent in both Battersbys in accent and approach, led to the siting of their factory in Runcorn, cannily taking advantage of the skilled workforce available in the wake of Plessey's redundancies there. Here they manufacture "anything that anyone is likely to use in the hardware side of the computer industry from one connector up to modems. We have even assembled the air-conditioning if that's what they want."

The finances are in good shape despite their dislike of having to be under a roof that is rented rather than bought. The 1986 turnover is expected to hit £2,750,000 with profit before tax of £322,000.

Bert and Rita are now attempting to expand the export side of the business and are finding that their approach works well: "We went out to the Far East to three large exhibitions and found that we could supply cable and connectors at a far better price than Japan or Taiwan could. That was a surprise, because you always hear that Britain is over-priced in markets like Singapore. We thought that we would go out and have a look with the idea that we could buy in some stuff from them."

"We looked at the prices at this exhibition in Singapore and realised that they were more expensive than us. So we reverted from buying to selling. It took us ten days to get an agent operating over there."

Now about 15% of their total sales are to the Far and Middle East, exporting cable made up to individual specifications.

Back in the UK the customer base continues to grow and so do the variety of services on offer. Rita says: "We do well because we complement the work that managers are doing. We are not going in and changing companies' ways of doing things. As a result, one of the nice things about the business is that we don't have irate customers."

As far as they are concerned there has been no great change in the business: "We are still doing the basic work, but we've grown with it so that we've been able to change quickly to suit individual customers."

VDUI effectively does not have one single largest customer. Out of 4,500 or so the Battersbys estimate the B&Q chain to be the one that keeps them busiest at the moment. They are also very proud of the work that they do for the National Westminster bank, who are VDUI's bankers.

"It took Rita seven years to get into the NatWest. They were the only bank we didn't do any work for, and they were our bankers, so there was a certain amount of repartee between us and our bank manager. Now we're doing a very complicated exercise for them in systems management which is another area where we've been growing in the past few years", smiles Bert. Typically even here their enthusiasm had run away with them: "We used to do it before for free but we are finally big enough to actually get paid for it now".

"As our skills continue growing we find that more and more people are asking for more and more skills from us. They say, 'hey, you've done a super job on that cabling — what about looking at this other problem we've got for you to sort out'. Rita keeps a tight rein on our financial resources so we can look at a new area and think whether we can offer a new service".

As far as Rita is concerned "the essence of it all is that we are constantly reforming and restructuring. You try and change as slowly as you can because introducing change is always difficult. At the same time you have to keep paddling like hell to keep with the pace".

Part of the challenge comes from having close on 100 employees. This has called on new skills to simply manage a business which is no longer Bert and Rita answering a telephone and getting the appropriate cables and connectors installed.

19

Again, their ability to keep it simple seems to be paying off: ''I like to think we've managed to motivate other people so that they can be successful and enjoy their job. You realise very early that if you want to grow you can't do it all yourself and you have to delegate. I recognised this the minute Bert joined. From it just being one person answering the telephone and doing everything, it became Bert answering the telephone as well. That was my first step in delegation. As the company grows it's quite challenging to learn to recognise talent and ability. You get a kick out of watching people growing in their job and achieving things, knowing that in one way their achievements are your achievements. In the end you are only as good as the management that you employ.''

The Battersbys retain a refreshing approach to figures and their accountant advisors. Rita has always been in overall charge of the financial direction of the company; she thinks that ''a lot of people take too much notice of what accountants say in as much as they can make you worry unnecessarily and make small businesses panic and make the wrong moves. Equally, I would never want them to change the role they fulfil: they are the monitors; they will give you the news and come and say to you 'oh dear, you are successful, you've got a tax problem' or 'oh dear, you haven't made it, do you still want to stay in business?'. What you have to remember is that they are not looking at the whole business so if you take too much notice of them they could ruin you.''

VDUI have used the small firm of Menzies, Middleton Hawkins to do their audit since 1980, and they take their tax advice from Price Waterhouse where partner, Barry Baldwin, who has made his name on a national basis as a small business advisor, looks after them. ''He is terrific'' says Rita. ''He's a one-off. Not really a strict accountant at all. He manages to bring commercial and entrepreneurial skill into it.''

This view of financial advisors as people who simply check the books, occasionally panic you into the wrong decisions and rarely possess the acumen of the average business manager, is one that tells you much about the nature of the Battersbys' success.

A similar attitude probably holds true for anyone who provides an ancillary service to the company. Rita and Bert know how to work the company. Outside offers of help are doomed to fail. After all, what could an outsider know of the way in which they do business?

It has meant that their progress, while financially successful, has been slow. That doesn't matter. They have taken each event or problem as it arrived, taken a good slow look at it, then worked out from their own internal resources of experience, expertise and common-sense what the answer should be.

Sometimes this has meant that as with the episode of the planning applications, they have not achieved intermediate goals. However, through what amounts to the awful old cliché of 'good housekeeping' they have kept the business providing the services that their customers need and relish.

The only remaining financial niggle they have is their new premises. After the fiasco of the derelict buildings, which could have become their offices and warehouse, they were forced to move into the new Bracknell building to house their expansion. Impressive it may be, but what rankles is the fact "we're paying £110,000 a year rent on a building that's owned by British Telecom's pension fund". That, to the Battersbys, makes no sense at all.

5

The next step for many businesses of this size and structure would be a move on to the Unlisted Securities Market. As one might expect, Rita and Bert are not absolutely sure about this.

They have put together a five-year plan, the first part of which was the move into the new building in Bracknell. As far as they are concerned the figures of their growth since then mean that they are on target to meet the plan's objectives. "The plan enables us to go to the USM, sell out, or continue as we are", Bert explains. The USM doesn't seem to hold much attraction for them. For a start they are greatly suspicious of the City. They doubt the merchant banks would understand their business and they certainly would have some problems

21

fitting the City's style into their way of thinking.

"There's no goal that says we have to go on to the USM in three years' time", Bert says. "The plan has to do with the company's natural growth anyway, and we have the feeling that the City may only be interested in quick bucks, only look at something which seems to them to be a high flier."

Rita is even less convinced. "The City", she proclaims, "is a bit conservative. They are into a quick buck situation and I don't think they would recognise us for what we are. It's a bit like schools. They look at historical information and from that they produce facts and analyse them. They're not in the marketplace looking at successful businesses. Added to that, we would be seen as either engineering or software. But we're not engineering and we're not software. We are a service industry which just happens to have a highly technical marketplace. They would find it very hard to assess what we were, and what our value in the market might be. They've not really got round to finding a slot that we fit into."

The one thing that does attract them to the USM is the fact that "it would mean our employees could have shares as could our daughters". The tradition of the benevolent family business could live on.

The other point that they are adamant about is, surprisingly, government help for small businesses. The Battersbys think it is both a waste of time and effort, and unnecessary. "We don't want government help", Bert declares. "We've never had it and we don't want it. Why should we use the tax payer's money to develop businesses?" Like many companies which have been resolutely independent, they feel that grants distort the efforts companies make and divert their attention from the main objective of keeping a clear eye on their market, their customers' needs and their development.

"What do government grants create?", asks Rita. "They create other companies to come in, set up for three years and then close down. A good idea to me would be no grants, no nothing, get a track record like we did, then when the day comes that you first start having to pay corporation tax you should be assessed. If you intend ploughing the profit back into the company for further growth, then you should be exempt from taxes." To the sophisticated financial observer much of this seems pleasantly naive. From where Rita and Bert stand, with a successful company grown around their talents and long hours of work, it all seems perfectly straightforward. It comes down to a view of common sense in the end.

Similarly the campaign against the people at local level who, the Battersbys feel, are out to thwart rather than assist small businesses. Bert equates it with the movement to roll back the domination and control by the unions in some areas of business life. "It's the same problem. If Maggie Thatcher can break the absolute power of the unions, why can't she get through to the local councils and all the Conservatives, who claim they are Conservatives but aren't really, like all the old colonels who hold this area to ransom. We are only one small company and like many others we are too busy developing our businesses so there will never be enough voices raised in protest. Successful people who are busy creating their own businesses haven't got the time to march on the streets of London."

Advice for anyone contemplating a future as an independent business is straightforward. Rita will initially lean back and emphatically say 'Don't'. Then she will reconsider and suggest that the snap judgement was unfair. But there is definitely a doubt there.

"It's very nice for me, having done it, to say that but I guess if I was in that person's shoes I would be doing it regardless of someone like me telling them not to."

"Armed with that advice, people should be committed and remember that they must never give up however tough it becomes and however many obstacles they find in their way. They should also be aware, which I certainly wasn't, that they will find themselves involved in politics. To me that was the biggest shock of all. You think you're purely going to run a business but you end up battling with local authorities and politicians. And that is sad."

Her doubts whether people should really get involved in starting a business from scratch, and then making it grow, are based on the stress involved. "You might not make it through because it is totally stress-related and it takes a lot of stamina. The commitment is vital. You have got to wake up every morning and say to yourself that I'm going to this today and I'm going to carry on for however long it takes and make it work. That hasn't been difficult for us in as much as we've never not wanted to do it. At the same time, your body will eventually say 'no' from time to time when you've really had enough. I've worked for 48 hour stretches and then just not turned up at dinner parties because I've fallen asleep.''

Rita admits there are times when she and Bert have wondered why they were doing it. "We didn't do it to make a lot of money. All we really did was set out to do something well. This may sound a bit naive but I do believe that if you want to do something very well then you are bound to be successful.''

In a curious way that says a lot about both Rita and Bert. They started with an idea born out of frustration at an industry blind to an opportunity, and they have very simply plugged away at it.

The overlay of sophistication which businesses gain as they grow is non-existent. They are very much the same Rita and Bert Battersby today as they must have been in the days when she was lugging cable into the Red Star parcel office, and he was coming home from IBM and sorting out what advice she should be giving the customers the following day.

They worked long and hard and they have never lost sight of why they are doing it. That is buried deep inside them and shows itself in their almost wrong-headed common sense and their resilience.

They are winners and they have done it in their own unique and quiet way.

SECOND WINNER: MICROVITEC

The story of Microvitec shows how a combination of great experience in a particular field plus a desire to run a new business can create a highly successful winning company. It is also the story of one man's enthusiasm and work. Tony Martinez is a small and energetic Spaniard who has spent nearly all his adult life in this country. His story shows that like Gio Benedetti, whose company won the Industrial Achievement award in 1985, the extra incentive of working in a country which is not your native land often provides greater competitive urgency.

The story of Microvitec also provides us with a more comprehensive picture of the growth of a company than any of the other winners. It is the only one so far to take the step of joining the Unlisted Securities Market. It is the only one which has consciously struggled to transform itself into a corporate maturity which means the entity itself becomes the main instrument of continuity rather than its founder and his team.

Of all the five winners, Microvitec has made the greatest effort to develop beyond a growing small business with a strong local presence. It is, if you like, rather further through its adolescence than the others. However, adolescence is a time when the line between triumph and disaster is at its thinnest. The fact that it is in the highly volatile microelectronics industry, making monitors and terminals, only makes its progress that much more fraught.

25

What Tony Martinez did, in the words of the offer document produced when they went onto the USM, was to 'recognise that, in spite of the growing demand for micro and personal computers and the substantial advantages offered by colour over monochrome in the presentation of information, there was no colour visual display monitor in production designed expressly for the microcomputer market, which was compatible with a large number of different systems and available at a competitive price'.

Put simply, Tony Martinez successfully identified a niche in the market, and proceeded to fill it. But it was a close run thing.

Microvitec won the Industrial Achievement award in 1982.

1

Despite his childhood on a farm in Malaga in the south-east of Spain, Martinez's background is in telecommunications. "I am third generation telecommunication engineer", he says. "My grandfather was a telegraph officer and my father was in both telegraphy and radio communications."

His family is Spanish as far back as he can trace, though he points out that south-east Spain is a great melting-pot of Mediterranean culture. His own particular part of that area was also 'a geological curiosity' and zinc, lead and manganese are mined there. His great-grandfather owned a mine. Another great-grandfather was a carpenter and all of his family were involved in local business, even his grandmother. She had an agency to sell dynamite to the mine.

Tony Martinez lived in Spain until he was 17. The town where his family worked was one of the first to fall to the Franco troops in the Civil War and he was moved to live with his grandmother in a town which held out against Franco almost to the end. Following Franco's victory Tony's father went into self-imposed exile, working for RCA communications in Tangier. The young Martinez and his brother joined him there in 1948.

"I worked as an apprentice to a teleprinter and morse operator and became very interested in telecommunications."

During these two years in Tangier he also had an English tutor. At school they had been taught French, German, Latin and Greek but 'amazingly enough', no English. "I got very fond of the language" and after two years he and his brother came over to England to study electronics.

They did what was then called a 'thick sandwich' course. "It was pretty intensive and the year that we were working in a factory we were also studying practically every evening," Martinez recalls.

After three years they both qualified and went their separate ways. His elder brother went off to work in Cambridge while Tony moved to Weybridge. This was the start of a career covering all the great names in British post-war electronics and which provided him with the mass of experience out of which his own brainchild would develop.

"The technology was very fast moving and the only way to keep up to date was a programme of continuous studying, working and making sure that you were involved in all the latest developments."

The first problem that he faced was the British industrial tradition of starting someone off as a skilled technician, only to force him along a career path which steadily dilutes his technical input and increases his purely managerial responsibilities.

This did not suit the young Martinez. "It was a natural progression. If you are an engineer you became an engineering manager and maybe if you are lucky, as I was, you take charge and become a chief engineer. If you stay on, you finish up being technical director. But I didn't like the idea of keeping to the one discipline."

Consequently he worked in a variety of companies. One of them developed the first transistorised radio receiver and the first portable battery-operated television. In another, he dealt with "some very fancy problems in closed circuit television broadcasting equipment". He worked in radar. Moreover, he gained the breadth of knowledge that he needed.

Finally Martinez made his first attempt to set up on his own. He started a small consultancy. "It was a very, very small business and I was really selling expertise. I was selling design time.'' This again proved useful later. He learned the difficulties as well as the satisfaction of working in a very small team. He gained more experience, particularly in designing colour television equipment for Marconi. However, he was not producing a product that could make a business grow.

So when Radio Rentals in Bradford approached him, he decided to move back into a larger company. ''They were just starting to get involved in colour television and were designing receivers and testing them. I talked with both the technical director and the chief engineer and they thought that with my consultancy work I could make a good contribution.''

''We came to a satisfactory arrangement which allowed me to finish off various contracts the consultancy business had outstanding while, at the same time, working for them. They had made me a good offer and going back to colour television work was very exciting for me at that time when there were quite a lot of new things happening.''

The consultancy experience he put aside for another time: ''I kept all the bits and pieces which I had in my laboratory. There was quite a lot of equipment which I had bought over a period of three or four years and I just locked it all up in my cellar. That equipment all came out again when I started Microvitec.''

He learned some valuable management lessons at Radio Rentals. Thorn had just taken it over, so it had become a larger organisation. It was the first time that he had properly made the transition from pure development to taking responsibility for other people. ''In British industry they don't train you to manage people. They just throw you at it and you either swim or sink. I had run the consultancy business, but here the challenge was very much bigger, the atmosphere very authoritarian in the sense that you had a lot of authority to carry out your responsibilities, and there were few questions asked as long as you had cleared everything with your boss. You were left to get on with your work and no one would question your decisions although I always tried to use the talents of the very large team we had there.''

"There were people there who had been in the company for many years and they were the leaders in their field." This was to prove vital later on, when the Thorn plant was closed down, and Martinez was looking for the brightest and the best for his new venture. "We were producing designs that, when launched, were the first world-wide. We were ahead of the Japanese," claims Martinez. He was appointed chief engineer of "what became one of the largest television manufacturing plants in western Europe. By the time I left in 1974 it was a pretty massive affair, employing around 4,500 people".

The blinkered path of engineers in management still annoyed him. In particular the type of information on which decisions were based: "I wasn't happy about how certain engineering decisions were made. I felt that there was something missing".

Martinez joined Texas Instruments which he found refreshingly different to anything he had done before. "I had some very funny kinds of jobs and did quite a lot of globetrotting. I did some marketing, talking to prospective customers and trying to identify the kind of products they were going to need two or three years down the line, then persuading the company to put in the investment so those products would be ready when they were needed."

His engineering background was important but he found also much of the new experience very exciting. "Although I made lots of mistakes, I also learned a lot". The travel involved gave him a new perspective on the industry and its markets, and provoked considerable thought. He concluded he ought to set up on his own. He was nearing 50 and he knew that what he was doing was not something he wanted to do forever.

Working in an American company made his mind up quicker: "I was 45 years old when I joined Texas Instruments. My experience was very good for what they wanted me to do. On the other hand, if one aspired to a very senior position in an American company, that was a very old age to join".

"I got this bee in my bonnet that I wanted to do certain things on my own. It just built inside like a crescendo, until I realised that if I didn't do something about it I was going to spend the rest of my life regretting I didn't have a go. If you have a go and it doesn't work then at least you can say to yourself 'at least I tried and it didn't work'. You will then be happier doing something else.'' He started planning.

2

Martinez took a firm engineering base as his starting point, and tried to develop ideas as to the kind of products he thought would be needed in the future. Part of his job at Texas was assessing opportunities emerging in the marketplace. His own plans ran in parallel.

"A lot of the work I was doing was related to specific components, and I was thinking along the lines of utilising these particular components in end equipment.'' He did try to interest people at Texas in some of his ideas. "But at that time they weren't the kind of things Texas was very interested in.''

The idea of his own company was by now firmly rooted. So as part of his planning he started to document exactly what he wanted to do. This was an important part of the early days of Microvitec. Most emerging businesses are under-planned and certainly under-documented. But he had picked up the habit from Texas Instruments and he was going to use it. "This is something you learn from American companies. You have to document your ideas, set them down in a logical manner, and give presentations to people. Communicating in that way is a discipline in itself. At the same time, it creates a methodology within your thinking. In a way you become the judge of your own programmes. You can measure whether what you are proposing makes sense.''

He did a lot of writing and documented the whole process fully. Then he decided to look for a partner. This took a while. His original choice as a partner went through a difficult period of divorce and remarriage only to take off for the US. Fortunately there was another Martinez brother, much younger than Tony, who was in Germany at the time and whose business plans were not working out. John Martinez came over, looked through Tony's plans, and eventually decided to come in as a partner.

Meanwhile Tony set himself a deadline of leaving Texas

Instruments by the middle of 1979, the following year. However, he and his brother decided to start earlier than planned and he left in April 1979. Between them they began the process of producing full documentation to ease the way towards gaining financial backing.

The problem was of taking engineering ideas and translating them into the language of venture capital. "It took a great deal of meetings, struggling to explain what we were trying to do. We had a pretty good idea of the costs of the equipment, how it was going to go together and how it was going to be designed. It was a question of trying to translate what were basically projections for equipment manufacture."

Tony found it easy enough to sort out the timescales they would be looking at. However, a financial plan with cash flow and profit forecasting involved extensive meetings and three or four months of fairly intensive work. "The final document contained a description of the financial plan, a description of the equipment and a breakdown of the cost. This was then restated in the form of a three year projection which covered start-up costs, the cash required and when the profit was going to start coming in."

In the meantime they had to fund themselves. "I have a large family with five children and if you are in engineering, even in a senior position, you don't really have a lot of money if you are educating your family and helping them with their careers. So I used to spend a lot of time decorating and having a quiet family life." He had bought a dilapidated property when he started work at Texas and in his spare time over the five intervening years had rebuilt and redecorated it. "I was very lucky, there was a housing boom at the time, and when I put it on the market it was worth three times what I had paid for it. So I was able to buy a much cheaper property in the North and I had cash I could put down as equity." John, his brother, had some savings. Hence they managed to survive the first few months while putting the plan together.

The next questions to be sorted out were where they would site their company and from whom they would get the financial backing.

At this point Thorn's operation in Bradford, (where Tony Martinez had previously worked,) was closing down, leaving behind a pool of highly experienced people in the microelectronics business. Recognising the potential of this labour force, Tony and his brother decided the city would make the perfect location for the company they hoped to create. "It was a very logical decision, but really Yorkshire had been my home for so many years, that of all the places I lived, this feels more like home than anywhere else". The family had very largely been brought up in Harrogate. Tony felt a particularly close association because of the children. "One of my lads became a professional footballer and used to play for Bradford City for a number of years."

Right from the start of his planning Bradford had always seemed the right place and in late 1978 Tony had paid a consultant to review the possibilities. However, what finally convinced him, over and above all other factors, was the reception they got when they took their plans to the Bradford Economic Development Unit. It proved to be the vital key to the success of the venture.

"The development unit had a tremendous vision and commitment which they put behind us". In fact, Martinez had decided that even if they failed to get the injection of finance then they were simply going to develop a workshop concept similar to the consultancy he had run before, but with some manufacturing facilities for proto-typing and sub-contracting.

Either route was possible with the backing of Bradford. Martinez agrees that moving to somewhere like Wales, or the North-East, would have given them a better financial package with a longer period of rate and rent-free concessions.

"But this kind of business is very much based on skill and it would have been difficult to find both the backing and the cluster of skills anywhere else. If you bring people in, then you have to start training them, and that can create huge problems."

On 6 July 1979 Microvitec was officially registered as a company. Back in June they had applied for financial backing from Technical Development Capital, a sister company of what was then the Industrial and Commercial Finance Corporation, now known as 3i (Investors in Industry).

ICFC were keen but wanted to strengthen the financial side of the embryo company. It approached a well-known local accountant, Iain Longman, who was not only a partner in the Leeds-based firm of Victor Walton, Croudson but also on the council of the Institute of Chartered Accountants. He agreed to act in an advisory capacity as part-time finance director of the company, joining the board officially in October 1979. ICFC came up with the money.

Longman recalls the euphoria of that time: ''It all seemed a marvellous idea but one which was very, very much in its early stages. I joined literally a week before they got the first money and they were really only buying the equipment and doing the first development work''.

''The great strength of the team they had created was that about 90% of them had worked at Thorn with Tony before, and had been unemployed since Thorn closed down. So when Tony came along offering work to people who had been highly skilled workers on a production line but who were now unemployed, or working at jobs like traffic wardens, they jumped at the chance and worked very long hours, putting everything in to the company for no extra special reward.''

''The main thing was that Tony Martinez had the vision to see a market for a particular type of product just at the right time, just when colour was coming in. We had time to do the development work and actually manufacture the product, if anything, slightly ahead of the market.''

Martinez decided that initially, while they were getting the work on the colour monitors under way, they should take on some other work just to keep the finances running. ''We had two or three minor projects which we felt would make us an initial living. Apart from basic sub-contracting, we were playing with small power supplies, which never really got anywhere, and solar heating controllers which did get us somewhere. At the same time, we were looking for a team of development engineers who could join us and start developing the products that we really wanted to go into production with.'' This initial development began at the end of 1979.

The cash raised totalled £250,000 with ICFC taking a third of the equity. Martinez was happy with that. He and his brother had put up £12,500 each with a commitment to putting in a further loan of the same amount later on. In the event, the money from John Martinez was never put in. Partnerships are difficult things in the early days of a business.

Tony Martinez was particularly pleased his loan was unsecured: "I personally felt this was very important. If anything happened to us and things didn't go well, then I still had a house and I could always get another job somewhere. From that point of view I didn't regard it as a very high risk personal venture."

The second tranche of money from his brother never materialised: "I don't know if it was the cause or the effect but the relationship was already beginning to become strained and it broke down very quickly after that." John Martinez left the company after a furious row in February 1981, during the first annual general meeting of the company.

Martinez feels there are important lessons to be learned from this breakdown of the partnership. "I think the thing one needs to stress to people who are starting companies is that, first of all, if the business is of some magnitude you can't do it on your own. You need a balance of skills. I had the engineering experience and I had some marketing experience but that meant we still needed commercial expertise in terms of sales and financial expertise."

"Partnerships in a start-up situation are very, very difficult. You have to know the person extremely well. You have to have worked with them for some time, and even then it's extremely risky. It is like a marriage going through a period of serious stress except the effects are more magnified. On top of this you have the pressures of cash flow, sales, production and future product development."

He reckons they were lucky the partnership broke up when it did. The company had made a £56,000 loss in that first year. The critical period of development, when the distractions of a partnership bust-up would have been crucial, was just ahead of them.

3

It was not until July of 1980 that Microvitec actually sold its first monitor. "We had sold a little bit of sub-contracting time and a few other bits and pieces, but that was the first time we actually produced a monitor which we sold to someone and got paid cash in hand."

Martinez is modest about the reasons for the monitors' success. He will cite luck, good timing and play down his own part: "When you measure your degree of brightness against other people, you always come out badly. There is always someone who is ten times more clever and has much more skill than you. If you think that you are a genius all you are really doing is standing up and allowing yourself to be counted as a bighead."

"It was a question of timing. There was an obvious need for something which was not a television receiver and something that was not a monitor in the way that they were understood in those days, when they were only used in broadcasting equipment and used for monitoring signals. Then they were very expensive and very accurate instruments. There was nothing available between these two concepts, so we tried to fill that gap."

When the Martinez brothers started the project in June, 1979, they had been to talk to the Department of Trade and Industry just to test out their ideas. They were mildly surprised to find they were greeted with enthusiasm. "Some of the guys there were really very knowledgeable about the industrial environment in which we were operating. We thought it was viewdata which was going to require a very cost-effective display. Although in the end business viewdata didn't really materialise."

Initially, Tony Martinez had planned to go into the original equipment manufacturer (OEM) market, selling the Microvitec monitor to other companies who could incorporate it into their products or own-brand it.

"That idea", recalls Iain Longman, "was very slow taking off. We had a lot of difficulty persuading people to change from green screens or black and white screens to colour."

Meanwhile, plans went ahead to ensure that if the idea did suddenly take off it would be possible to produce sufficient monitors to cope with demand.

"We knew the most critical phase would be the changeover from developing the products to actually producing them in quantity", says Martinez. "So we undertook some sub-contracting work, making solar heating controllers for a firm in Wales. This way we were able to build up the production capacity which we needed to make the transition."

To start with they aimed to build what they called an LCCD, a low complexity colour display. This was designed to be a universal chassis. Companies buying it could use it for all manner of different products depending on what they put around it or how it was interfaced with other equipment. Martinez was uncertain about it initially: "We built it in a form that meant in some markets it was too good to compete and was perhaps not good enough to compete in others." Hence the problems of getting into the OEM market.

However, with that stroke of luck and timing in which Martinez believes so strongly, they were saved from a most unlikely quarter.

"Suddenly the craze for Space Invaders games came along. Not only did they want exactly the basic concept we had created, they also wanted the size of monitor to which we were committed. They just went crazy on the idea of the 14 inch chassis which they could build into big machines and put a lot more hardware into."

"In a very short space of time, we went from being a company with a very low base, doing bits and pieces here and there, selling a few different shapes and sizes, into a company which had suddenly found a big market queueing up outside the door to take our product."

Like so many fashionable fads, it created a frenzied period of growth. Virtually 90% of production was devoted to making monitors for Space Invaders machines. Then after six to nine months it died away. However, in that short period, it provided sufficient revenue to fund further development. The OEM market started to pick up and then Microvitec was swept along with another sudden growth in interest. Once again the impetus again came from the youth market, but this time it was the Government which created it rather than amusement arcades and pubs.

The programme to flood Britain's schools with micro-computers, making them a familiar part of every schoolchild's life, leaned very heavily on Microvitec's ability to build a cheap, cheerful, and above all robust monitor which could carry the colour graphics that children could revel in.

"We talked to a number of education authorities and they were just becoming involved in micro-computers. Again, they wanted something which was not a television receiver nor an expensive monitor."

"They wanted something which would look like a piece of equipment and which children would respect. They could never respect a television receiver in that way. Our product was much better in quality and reproduction, yet not very expensive. It was very rugged and made of metal because it had to be fireproof. It just happened to be ideal for the classroom."

The gearing up for the volume of production needed was not as difficult as it might have been. Having scooped up the experience of his old Thorn colleagues and employees, Martinez had a team used to setting up products right the way through from design to production line. They had done it all before. The only difference was that they were working for a company in a small team environment.

Martinez wanted to experiment with more than just technical ideas in his company. "We had to try and create a new industry, but it was not only the product but also the way in which we did it which was important. We decided from the outset that Microvitec would be an equal opportunities company."

"If an industrial environment is going to be part of our lives, then it has to be as democratic as life has been outside of industry in Britain for many years. The democratic environment you find in Britain has not been reflected in British industry."

In an attempt to rectify this, Martinez set about creating a work structure in which everybody is encouraged to participate. Initially meetings of the whole work-force were held to discuss the company's progress. However, it was later felt that more could be achieved through the use of works committees.

Good lines of communication are an essential feature of the company, and a simple management structure means there is normally only one level of management beneath the chairman. By maintaining this structure Martinez hoped that, as the company grew in size, the sense of belonging could be preserved.

He was also very aware of the individual needs of the employees. "We were keen to make sure the individuals felt that what they were doing in the organisation, as well as being of benefit to the company, was also part of their own development and growth".

Martinez is quick to recognise success is very much a reflection of team effort. He is a very powerful driving force himself, but he readily acknowledges the invaluable contribution made by the rest of the workforce.

Much of this philosophy stems from the very early days of the company when they were realising that, as a company, they had their own unique problems and necessarily had to sort them out for themselves.

"The difficulties began when we had to start product diversification. We had to develop many more products which were not quite the same and therefore required a lot more start-up resources in terms of people, money, space and talent. Moreover it all had to come together at the same time."

The lessons learned at this time were very important, but most important of all was the transition from what Martinez sees as a workshop environment into a corporate structure.

"In 1980, when we first moved in, we had 30 people in 12,000 square feet. The whole company was in what I call the 'workshop stage'. You could stand up and see the whole enterprise. In one area we were assembling, in another we were doing the development work. We had a little desk that was purchasing, another that was general administration. You could literally stand up and see the whole company.''

"You could see the complete problems and divert your resources instantly if you suddenly needed to. If a new delivery arrived you could say, 'Come on lads, we have to unload that van', and everyone would stop their work and unload that van.''

"The next minute the phone would ring and someone would say, 'You promised me 30 units by tomorrow'. I would say, 'Hey guys, we've got to get those 30 units off. Nobody goes home tonight until they get packed'. At that stage it's very easy to communicate with people and create team spirit because everything is so tightly balanced. You break for lunch and take your sandwiches to a little seat in the corner. There's a little table and sink unit to make tea for everybody. It's dead easy.''

"But as soon as you build another room next door, and you don't see everyone all the time every minute of the day, then your communication path length increases. From that time onwards you have to do everything differently.''

For people who have worked all their lives in large companies where an organisational structure and pattern have been laid down, this transition can be difficult. It is very different expressing one's individuality by subtly twisting or changing a large company's practices to finding oneself initiating the whole pattern with a small team. "When you start from zero there simply isn't a package you can buy and say, 'that is what our organisation guide will be from tomorrow, what our tradition will be'.''

Martinez happily admits they had a disaster every day: "The biggest problem was firefighting. You spend so much time firefighting on a day-to-day basis that tempers get short, people start shouting at one another and the one thing you haven't got time for is to sit down and say, 'Hey guys, what do we have to get sorted out which aren't day-to-day things, so tomorrow we won't have to firefight so much?' ''

Microvitec eventually reached a stage where planning could take greater priority. However, before that the company went through several cash crises: "Buying colour tubes for the monitors was very hard. If you wanted to start buying them in bulk, even now, you would find it very, very difficult. It's just one of those things, for some reason colour tubes are a very closed club.''

''People don't usually supply colour tubes to anybody else because they are very expensive items — it is hard, initially, to gain the confidence of suppliers so they believe they will get paid. Moreover, many suppliers are potentially in competition in the manufacture of monitor products.''

Martinez eventually persuaded a manufacturer to supply: ''But when you buy tubes you can't buy them in ones and twos. You have to buy them in container loads. Even a 20 foot container is worth over £30,000.''

By the time the second container was on its way they were already short of cash, wondering how they could meet the 30 day payment deadline. They went back to ICFC. This was in the middle of the row between the two Martinez brothers so things were even more difficult than they should have been.

''We said we needed another £70,000. They looked at the fact we were already selling and reasonably profitable. So they stuck their neck out and gave us a short-term loan. Then we went to the bank and worked out another loan, but because we were so desperately short of cash I was looking to over-the-counter trading to sell 10% of the company to a broker. After much discussion they came out with a deal to issue shares and sell the 10% for £120,000. That valued the company in July 1981 at £1.2 million and was a much needed breakthrough because we were literally starving for cash at the time.''

This created a tripartite shareholding — 30% each for the two brothers and ICFC, with the remaining 10% placed in newly issued shares.

The idea of relinquishing even part-ownership of their project was a difficult one to come to terms with. However, the cash-flow problems taught them the importance of being able to grasp opportunities as and when they arise.

''Obviously, you would like to retain complete control, but you have to develop a relationship whereby you share the ownership simply because if you don't, then you will always

40

be starting from a very, very small base. So even if you are very, very successful it will take you a long time to grow.''

"Unfortunately, in high technology this is almost impossible. High technology has opportunity windows which open up at different times, and you have to be able to take advantage of them. You have to deliver a lot of products into certain markets at a certain time. If you don't have the capabilities to do that, then you just fail miserably.''

Martinez's assessment is well illustrated by his competitors' experience. "At that particular time about six monitor manufacturers sprang up in the UK. They all wanted to get into this market. But when you look around now there is really only one left, other than Microvitec. That one was doing small volume work ten years before we came into the market. And they are still doing exactly what they were always doing — very specialised work, in very small volume for a very high price."

4

Microvitec's priority has always been one of growth. The first months of existence up to the end of 1980 saw a pre-tax loss of £56,000 on turnover of £189,000. In the first full-year's trading turnover swelled to £1,375,000 with a pre-tax profit of £158,000. The following year, the key year of 1982, saw turnover almost double to £2,671,000 with pre-tax profits up to £195,000.

1982 was an important year, the year when they became universally recognised as winners. The Microvitec team won the Industrial Achievement award sponsored by *Accountancy Age* and Lloyds Bowmaker. They also won an award sponsored by merchant bankers, Hill Samuel, who were seeking to commemorate their 150th anniversary by making an award to a small, newly established business.

The two awards brought in £40,000 in prize money, but they also provided a degree of recognition in the marketplace, an improved perception of Microvitec as a serious company with long-term growth potential. "Winning the Industrial Achievement award," said Martinez, "had a very significant

41

impact for the company. We were now recognised where we hadn't been before. Now our name was known all over the country.''

Winning the Hill Samuel award gave them something else, contact with a merchant bank for the future: "They were looking at companies that were one day going to go onto the USM and who would be looking for a merchant bank. So they kept talking to us, and eventually we said, 'look, come and talk to our board, give us a presentation. We will then give you a presentation about our plans. You can look at that in detail, then tell us whether we are ready to go to the USM or not'.''

Microvitec had decided quite early on that some sort of listing was going to be essential. In that sense it had always been part of the plan.

''We had years of experience in the company and we all had a very clear understanding of the business. However, once we started putting projections together we kept finding ourselves saying, 'you can't do this because we're going to be short of production space. You can't do that because we're going to be short of cash'. We knew we couldn't keep growing and diversifying without a massive cash injection.''

There was a feeling that the whole enterprise was getting on top of its management, despite new operational directors being brought in. ''It was not a job anymore. It was a vocation. You get up in the morning with it. You live with it throughout the day. You get up in the middle of the night and make a little note about something that has just occurred to you, because you know that if you don't then you won't get back to sleep again. It's your job all the time, weekends and Sundays. When you go for a walk you still have a little notebook in your pocket so that you can write down an idea when it comes to you.''

At the same time, they were wary of outside advisors. They were worried they would not be able to judge effectively enough whether the news and advice they might be given was something they should follow, modify or ignore.

Finally they decided the best method was to bring someone in on their own internal understanding that they would follow the advice. ''We were not going to bring an expert in to look at Microvitec, try to develop that understanding, listen to what they told us and, then, if we didn't like that advice say we wouldn't follow it."

At this point, Hill Samuel arrived on the scene.

For a company which knows inside out what goes on in a circuit board and which is mainly staffed by exceptionally bright and enthusiastic engineers, the whole business of bringing in the City experts and going for a listing was daunting. Suddenly they were faced with having to trust people from a totally different discipline, and taking the ways of the City of London into account, from virtually a totally different world.

"The City is a kind of maze to anyone who doesn't know his way around. From our point of view, as a little workshop company as we were then, it was awe-inspiring and frightening. It's a different language, the way they are always so polite and very constrained, how no one ever gets excited about anything. Even now, I still don't understand everything that happens there by any means."

Despite this gulf of culture and experience, there was an important bond for Martinez: "The people we were talking to were individuals, and you develop a relationship with individuals, learn to communicate with them. You try and learn their language, and they learn yours, so that after a few meetings you don't find it a problem any more. Every so often you meet two of them together and learn a new word. You have to go off and find out what it means. You just have to play it by ear. But in the end it wasn't too difficult."

The other major stumbling-block is the different viewpoint each side has of the company and its purpose: "For someone who has been involved in industry throughout his life it is important to understand, very early on, that the City sees a company purely in terms of an investment."

"For them it is not much different from going to the races and backing a horse. Whereas to you, you've dedicated your whole life to something you have always wanted to do. You want it to do well, to develop a good reputation and you want it to stay successful. To you it's not an in and out thing. To

43

the people that invest it can be.''

''The attitude is one of 'I'll back you today but if tomorrow I don't fancy you, or I fancy someone else more than I fancy you, I'll take the money out from here and put it there'. It is strange, and it has nothing to do with any experience you can relate to.''

To someone who believes in the wider importance of business, it was obviously very difficult to understand. Martinez makes a point about the City's lack of emotion: ''When you are talking about your life, and the lives of the people working in the factory, then obviously it's very emotional and you can't divorce yourself from it. Whether you hide your emotions or express them, or dress them up as something else, they are there with you all the time. To the City it's perhaps less emotional because they are doing this type of work every day.''

The figures for the year to 31 December 1983 provided the impetus required. Turnover was up from £2,671,000 to a staggering £9,614,000 and pre-tax profit leapt from £195,000 to £2,513,000. In one year pre-tax profit had almost managed to eclipse the previous year's turnover. It was a tremendous achievement by any standards.

The key to it lay with the Department of Industry's 'Micros in Schools' campaign. Martinez was able to point out in his chairman's statement in the report and accounts which appeared in early 1984, that the monitors they were supplying to the scheme were then used in over 20,000 schools by more than two million schoolchildren.

This was the start of the memorable adventures which were finally to take Microvitec onto the USM. However, it was not the sort of profit growth that could be maintained once the schools' programme was fully equipped with monitors. The original finance director, Iain Longman, explains: ''Profitability was very high in the early days and mainly influenced by Government policies. You got a very good margin in the educational sector, but once you got into the OEM market then you were not going to be able to maintain that. People like IBM and ICL are not going to give you a 28% gross profit margin.''

"So you accept lower profit margins. On the other hand it's a much safer business, and that was where the real future was going to be. The educational market was full of peaks and troughs. If they had any money left then you'd always get a rush in February and March, and then no orders again until about July, because they'd got to spend the rest of their budget."

As with the early boom from the Space Invaders craze, the education market provided Microvitec with cash to re-invest, assuring its real future. The team grew, and Martinez made sure their contribution was always emphasised. In the 1983 report he noted, "This performance has been due to the Microvitec team, their talent, and above all their dedication and commitment to the company. Our equal-opportunity, equal-status philosophy is as much part of our company and our team as the products which we make and the customers we serve."

In a press interview at the time he underlined the importance of communications: "The people here believe in what they are doing", he stated. "Communications are easy, everyone is kept informed of what we are doing and we all pull together to achieve our objectives. The enthusiasm here is transparent and contagious. We all appreciate that we can only get out what we put in. Engineering is more about people than engineering." In 1982 Martinez had established an independent trust which held shares for employees so that all employees could have a shareholding in the company.

The decision to accept Hill Samuel's advice to go onto the USM was taken in the opening weeks of 1984. The Microvitec board argued for an early listing. Hill Samuel argued caution. It was to be May before they reached the stock market in what turned out to be the best debut of the year.

The sheer cost of dealing with all the City experts deemed necessary to introduce a company to the markets often deters the wary amongst small businesses. However, for Microvitec the costs, although large, were both containable and accurate.

"We had all the costings spelt out and everyone involved gave us their commitment. So we knew exactly how much it was going to cost. In the end the figures came very, very close.

There was a bit allowed for contingencies, and in two instances the split differed from the original plan, but overall the total cost came very close indeed to the original budget.''

Martinez thinks, unlike some critics of the City, that the cost was certainly worth it. "There's no doubt it is an expensive affair. Unless the money that's going to come back into the company's coffers is a reasonable sum, which means the expenditure incurred is a small proportion of that sum, then it is not worth doing. You can't go to the market and make it worthwhile if you are only going to raise £1 million or so, unless you do it on a sort of over-the-counter deal.''

Iain Longman agreed: "It was the cheapest way for the company to raise additional finance. It was getting short of production space as well as working capital to finance its growth, especially if it was really to develop its export market. Without the USM it was always going to have to be borrowings from the bank, and we were always going to be owing ICFC money. The USM seemed to be the answer to a lot of the problems at the time.''

A year which was to see both triumphs and disasters was well under way.

Like many other aspiring USM companies, Microvitec changed its auditors. At the time they were still with the firm of accountants which had put the original finances together mostly dealing with just one person.

Eventually they were hived off to the audit firm's Liverpool office and Tony Martinez felt the lack of personal understanding and experience of Microvitec's affairs was not good for their relationship with the auditors.

At the same time, Hill Samuel had suggested (in November 1983) that it would be worth getting another firm of accountants in — to do a report on Microvitec's long-term prospects with an eye to the USM entry.

Peat Marwick came in to do that report and, in the way of these things, they eventually took over the audit. They have been a great success. "The question of your relationship with your auditors is terribly important. Sometimes it works and sometimes it doesn't, but with Peat Marwick it has worked out very well," endorses Martinez.

It is often not realised, until far too late, that the whole process of gaining a listing is immensely time-consuming. Microvitec failed to realise this at the time and were to pay dearly for the error of judgement. The worst part is that with a small company everyone with any clout and expertise in the company is sucked into the process.

Iain Longman sums it up graphically. "The actual mechanics of going to the USM with a small management team cost the company very dearly."

"There were three or four months of intensive work for the full-time executives with all the meetings in London. Initially Hill Samuel insisted everything had to be done down in London, and it was only in the later stages they started coming up here for meetings. But in the first half of that year the company didn't have the time, with hindsight, and certainly didn't spend enough time developing the company's products."

"Then there was a quick period of euphoria, which was great. It was the USM's biggest-ever over-subscription at the time. It really didn't hit them until July or August. Then everyone suddenly realised, my God the company's going down the nick again."

Martinez feels that, of all the lessons he has learned in his brief independent business career, this is the most important of all.

"I think that if you repeated it over and over again 20 times it would not go amiss. Remember young companies have small organisational structures with all their directors as operational directors. If you are all already working 70 hours a week, and you decide to go public, where do you get the time from? You have to take all your directors and spend a tremendous amount of time with solicitors, accountants, merchant bankers and brokers. It is an extremely time-consuming affair."

"If you like you can define it by quantum of management. If you have a very clever guy in the company then maybe that one person can have the quantum. Usually you have a number of people and they all have parts of the talent that goes to make up that company's quantum."

"Now, if you take all of this quantum of management and you lock them up in a room for hours on end, day after day, what you are doing — but rarely do people recognise it — is taking that amount of quantum away from the management of the company."

"The company is seen to go on to a great success. It was said that the Microvitec launch was probably the most successful the City has ever had, but when we came back the company was no longer the same. We had lost three months of operational management guidance and drive and that caused irreparable damage."

The problem is also that the whole process is obviously a fascinating and exciting one for the managers of the company. It is very hard — having already identified that throwing oneself wholeheartedly into a particular idea is what produces success — not to find yourself completely wrapped up in learning about all these new disciplines and ideas, spending all your available time bringing the plans to fruition.

Martinez is convinced the results are the same but to the detriment of the company's future. "Our original plan was to raise £3½ million and to value the company at £35 million. In the event we got more than £4 million. But the extra million we got out of the USM is what we missed out of profits."

"It was the same quantum. You either put it to do this or you put it to do that. Without thinking, we chose USM effort rather than company at that time."

The other problem, of course, is that it is not a lesson many people are willing to learn beforehand. "That is perhaps the biggest danger. I refused point-blank to believe that this was time-consuming because they had told us we would have to issue this document or that document."

"I thought, well, with all the reports and projections I have written in my life, I could knock one of these out over a weekend. If I really get up early on a Saturday and work right through it will be finished by Sunday night."

To the vigorous company director this sounds straightforward enough. It doesn't work that way: "It took three bloody months and at times there were 20 people round the table with all the directors working until 10 o'clock at night.''

''When we first started talking to them we thought they were a bunch of wankers. All these City gents, we would say, what the hell do they know about industry. But after we had worked with them for a few weeks we had learned an awful lot from them. They were a bunch of real professionals. They had done it all before and nothing was going to escape them.''

''Even a simple, straightforward issue like ours, where there weren't any great complications, took three solid months of hard work. We learned to respect their kind of professionalism and we hope they learned a little bit about our kind of professionalism in our industry.''

For Iain Longman, the overall lesson for anyone taking the same route is that they must do it, but they must plan: ''I think you've got to go through a USM experience but realise that, although people warn you it will take up a tremendous amount of management time, it will take up far more time than anyone can ever tell you. Moreover, there isn't time to do that and run a business. Unless you can somehow plan it, your business is going to suffer.''

On the day over 100,000 applications came in for the shares. They were oversubscribed by 37.6 times and allocations were scaled down accordingly.

Yet probably the most important fact was that 212 of the applications were from employees. These were accepted in full. It meant that over 90% of the workforce were shareholders.

The first day of trading was, according to Iain Longman, a bit of an anti-climax after that. Their brokers, Greenwells, took them onto the floor of the Stock Exchange on the first day. ''We were not'', he observes, ''the same sort of attraction as the Pineapple Dance debut, but it was an interesting experience.''

''They took us back into their box afterwards, and that was what brought the whole thing home to me most. Watching them at work you realise the only people who can really make money on the Stock Exchange are the people on the floor of the exchange.''

"I thought to myself, 'the chap even on the outside in London hasn't got a cat in hell's chance'. You saw people in Greenwell's box buying and selling their shares over a five or ten minute span. They were in and out and they've made their profit. All the ordinary punter would see is a price in the paper the next day and wonder to himself should or shouldn't he buy. I can see why people in the City make more in capital gains than they do on their salaries."

From its USM debut, like it or not, Microvitec and its share price were items for public interest and public comment. Understandably, but again with hindsight not so sensibly, the company pulled in its horns. The shares went to the market at 180 pence, briefly rose to 210 pence, then spent the rest of the year falling.

The company stuck to its plans. Orders and organisation might have fallen away during the USM experience but the original reasons for raising the money had not. There was a new factory to be built and an export market to be chased. Recognition had already come in the month prior to the listing in the form of a Queen's Award for technological achievement.

Martinez is candid about the post-USM period. "Everyone loves you. You are in all the newspapers and you get a little bit blinded by all the publicity. Instead of being a pumpkin you become a Cinderella. Nobody had spotted the problems."

"Neither the brokers nor the merchant bankers ever said to us, 'Guys, who's running the company while you're all here?' ".

Martinez feels that what ultimately saved them — apart from the obvious routes of bringing in more and better management and getting the new factory organised for greater production — was financial conservatism. As a result they managed to live through the crisis.

"A lot of companies, like Acorn for example, found when they turned round again that the company was gone and someone else had to come and bail them out."

"We have always taken the view that this is a job for life. The company needs its resources and you are not going to take them out for your own use. From that point of view our accounting has always been very conservative and we haven't had any luxuries. We have never had any Rolls-Royces or anything like that because we felt the important thing was to survive.''

"If you survive and keep growing then anything you may need as a person becomes a very small proportion of the total. When what you are taking out is a measurable proportion of the total, then it will have an adverse effect on the business.''

He regrets now that the attempt to change from a workshop to a corporation, as far as their organisation model was concerned, was made later than it should have been. They should have developed an organisation which would have sustained the change. And they hadn't.

"We came back, just after the summer holidays and we had to say, 'guys, we're just not going to do it. The projection we had for profits this year is just not going to happen'. Then we started to pack an awful lot of things into a very short period of time. Yet it just didn't work. We fell short of our targets.''

"We were exploding the company in terms of volume, in product diversity, in product complexity. We needed many, many more engineers to provide support in both production and design. Everything had to be managed extremely well. Our management information system was frankly non-existent.''

They had made the error with financial staff in not ensuring enough industrial accounting expertise was on site. They had made great improvements in bringing in budgetary control but had failed to ally this with a very detailed management information system.

"So we worked for almost a year, from mid-1984 to mid-1985, when there were variances coming up in the accounts that we couldn't understand. Consequently, some of the decisions we made to take corrective action were in the wrong direction.''

Even at this late stage it was difficult for successful engineers to see quite what needed to be done. It took a lot of boardroom ructions before a new finance director, with a wealth of relevant experience, was appointed. "He had tremendous experience of cost accounting and started to develop management information systems that could tell us precisely what was happening. In the middle of 1985 we started to be able to take corrective action.''

"It took a long time before it started to have any effect. Certainly the business was very different at the end of 1985 to what it had been at the end of 1983. These were two years of transition, and profitability went simply because neither the organisation nor the system were good enough to support the level of business we were doing.''

5

For the year to the end of 1984 the turnover continued to climb. It grew from the 1983 figure of £9,614,000 to £14,806,000 but pre-tax profit moved hardly at all. 1983 pre-tax profits had swelled to £2,513,000. For 1984 pre-tax profits all but stagnated at £2,640,000. In his chairman's statement, Tony Martinez commented that this was 'disappointing and below expectations'. The share price which had fallen as low as 57 pence, started a slow recovery.

For the team at Microvitec the whole business of having a share price as a public measure of success and failure was new, and they were somewhat sceptical.

They find they take note of how it is doing but try not to let it influence them too much. They try to stick to the distinction between what they feel a fair valuation of the company really is, and the share price as only a perception of what the value should be. They accept that sometimes the perception is right and sometimes it is wrong.

The added stress this can create surfaced just before the end of 1985.

Immediately prior to Christmas the share price suddenly started to collapse dramatically. At one brief point it fell as low as 18 pence. The figures for the share price over the year showed Microvitec as one of the worst performers with a fall of 76%. Tony Martinez was baffled at the final plunge. There seemed to be no rational explanation.

"The company was still growing. We knew what our cash

position was and we were still strong. The asset ratio was still strong. Our only real weakness was that we were overstocked but there was nothing there we knew we couldn't convert into cash by putting a plug on it, and selling it.''

Martinez was in Spain seeing his father just before Christmas when the news came through. ''My broker rang and said: 'Tony, what the hell is going on?'. I said that as far as I knew there was nothing going on. 'The company's going well. We're still going to meet the figures that the City expects and there aren't any skeletons in the cupboard anywhere.' ''

''He then said to me, 'well, the share price is just collapsing and there are now a number of shares that no one is prepared to buy. The brokers are just marking them down.' So I told him to start buying them, because if someone is prepared to give them away then I am prepared to buy them.'' Between then and the end of the year Martinez and fellow directors bought over 300,000 shares. The price recovered but the mystery of the fall remained.

It was only at a dinner in January that Martinez discovered, through a casual conversation, what had happened.

''It was all to do with credit insurance. We have credit insurance on our customers and some of our suppliers have credit insurance on us. It's a very closed club and apparently someone had made a comment that Microvitec had not paid a bill, so must be in financial trouble. It turned out that in fact it wasn't Microvitec at all, but one of our customers. However, the fact Microvitec was mentioned had obviously created all the panic. One big shareholder had put a large holding of shares on the market and people wouldn't buy them.''

Martinez thinks the whole saga is a ridiculous example of how perceptions fail to take the company's resources into account. Although he also happily admits that when they went to the market they were in no way worth the price-earnings ratio placed on them.

1985 was still a year when troubles were being tackled and problems ironed out. Turnover doubled and pre-tax profit halved. From turnover of £14,810,000 Microvitec leapt to

£29,740,000. In contrast pre-tax profits of £2,640,000 slumped to £1,150,000. The share price hovered around 35 pence.

Martinez admits that they have still not got it right. He and others in the company wear a badge which carries the motto 'Right on time'. It is all part of the efforts they make to ensure that motivation leads to quality and cost-effective production.

The new factory is there, Princess Anne opened it in late 1984. The whole place is clear, clean and efficient in appearance. There is an enthusiasm amongst the workforce. The whole place is friendly. Tony Martinez is addressed as Tony by everyone. There is an obvious loyalty to someone who has tried as hard as he has and is so transparent in his emotional response to events and people.

He believes the new products are what the market wants. The Micro Graphics subsidiary, producing terminals, grew 400% last year and Martinez is quick to point out the profitability on terminals is much higher than monitors. "We have put a lot of investment into our products and some of the new products are beginning to pay off," he concludes. And the analysts agree. Brokers Capel-Cure Myers, for example, put out a report to their clients in April 1986 headed 'Microvitec-Recommendation: Recovery Buy'. 'Microvitec', the first paragraph read, 'is at last on the road to improved profitability.'

Microvitec is now the largest colour monitor manufacturer in the UK as well as the UK's largest colour terminal manufacturer. Martinez will claim to be not just the market leader but the technology leader and pins his faith in that fact providing the profits of the future.

Exports rose from £100,000 in 1983 to £1 million in 1984 and £2.4 million in 1985. The number of employees in unemployment-battered Bradford is 350. The hope is that they are now pushing through into a new maturity with the past workshop environment run by a dominant chairman supplanted by a fully-fledged corporation, which still runs to Martinez's influence.

"I have to reconcile myself with my own temperament, in a way make myself redundant. The worst thing that could

54

Bert and Rita Battersby of VDU Installations

Tony Martinez of Microvitec

happen would be if Tony Martinez was seen to be Microvitec, and Microvitec was seen to be Tony Martinez. It has never been like that. I've obviously made a contribution but we do have an extremely strong and talented team.''

The change to a system where the original tightly-knit team no longer runs everything is a difficult one. "I have to learn a different job now. You can't run it like a workshop anymore. You can't be everywhere. Sometimes you feel like you want to go to a particular department and get involved, but you have to stand back and just say to someone, 'Have you thought about so and so?' and get them to realise what you want to see happen. Or maybe I go in with a false impression and say to someone, 'Have you thought of so and so?' and they say 'Yes, didn't you realise that we'd thought about it?' and you come back. And you have learned a lesson.''

"Engineers need to be motivated and driven because they are a special breed of people. They are creative yet they have to be self-disciplined because they tend to fall in love with their creations. It is difficult in a commercial environment to keep that balance.''

It has obviously been hard to move into a management structure where the chairman has to work out who is the right person to direct a particular division rather than sorting out the circuits. The painful decisions Martinez finds the hardest: "My biggest weakness is that I can't tell people off. If I have to do that I will go round the block for half an hour, then come back, sit down and write it out and say to myself, 'Is that what I want to say?'. Then I'll sit with the chap and tell him''.

"On the other hand, I find it easy to pat people on the back when they've done something right and let it be known they have done something worthwhile. That I find very easy to do. I find more pride in doing that.''

His advice to anyone thinking of starting up a business is relatively simple. "If you feel you have a contribution to make and that contribution warrants setting up a business, and you are committed enough, then you should do it.''

"Most people have more talent than they give themselves credit for. Perhaps where they fall short is that they put a limit

55

to the amount of effort they believe is needed to achieve something. If you really want to achieve something then you can't count the effort."

His greatest fear has been to feel that he has not done as much as he could. Other things matter less: "If someone says 'Tony, you're talking through the back of your neck' and someone proves it to me, then I will say 'you're right'. Being wrong is human. All the biggest mistakes in this company have been made by me."

"But the thing I hate is not being successful. If it takes every atom of my energy to achieve something, and I really want to achieve something, then I'll do it. If I drop dead in the process that's exactly what I wanted to do, so why not do it."

"If you don't think it's worthwhile to that extent then don't start it. Do something else. But if you think it's worthwhile, don't count the hours. You're going to need not just every amount of energy but all the time you have. You're always going to be short of time. That's essential."

Martinez now has a pleasant house in the Yorkshire countryside. He counts as his only real luxury a custom-built dining table large enough to get his entire family — children, grandchildren and all — round it on Sunday lunchtimes.

Tony Martinez has been given a doctorate by Bradford University and an OBE from the Queen. His achievements have made him as pleased as Punch.

THIRD WINNER: NORFROST

The story of Norfrost's business success is little short of amazing. Anybody asked to bet on the likely outcome of an enterprise set up a stone's throw from John O'Groats, in the far north of Scotland, with the intention of becoming a high volume, low cost maker of domestic freezers, would be likely to keep their hand firmly in their pocket.

Yet Norfrost, the result of an unlikely alliance between an electronics-mad son of a crofter and a Teesside woman in the air force, not only managed it quite happily but succeeded in turning what seemed overwhelming adversity into a substantial element of its success.

With its nearest customer 300 miles away, its closest competitor 500 miles away, Norfrost automatically built self-sufficiency into its plans. Problems for which other manufacturers had simple answers required different solutions. Its founders were forced to apply ingenuity, enthusiasm and hard work in a way their competitors did not.

The result was the sort of success that only comes when people allow their talents to burgeon.

Norfrost was the winner of the Industrial Achievement award in 1983.

1

Norfrost was the brainchild of husband-and-wife team, Pat and Alex Grant. Alex comes from a local crofting family, one

57

of eight children. Pat comes from a family of nine living in a council house in Stockton-on-Tees. They met at a dance in Wick when Pat was up on holiday with an air force friend.

Alex Grant discovered electrical engineering as a boy. An engineer from Glasgow had retired to a house nearby, and Alex started to spend his weekends and evenings at his workshop. "He had a very good knowlege of electrical wiring, repairing radios and even cars."

"As a boy of about seven years old I got to know all about cars and motor bikes. When I was 10 years old I had a small scooter which I completely stripped down and rebuilt with his assistance. It was two-stroke and I knew all about valves, pistons, sparking plugs and all the rest of the kit that goes with small motor bikes."

"I learned all about radio with him then went to a Sutherland technical school. It was based purely on technical education. All the students there got woodwork, metal work, and engineering drawing. It was all technical subjects, there was no emphasis on history or any of the arts". The school has long since been closed "because of this comprehensive system they brought in".

"The director of education would get more money if they closed that school down and combined it with another. It was as cynical as that", says Alex. He is not happy about the way engineers are treated in this country.

Pat Grant had an equally practical childhood. Her father had his own upholstery business when she was young. "He used to take me to his workshop a lot, I used to sit there passing him nails and bits and pieces. I thought it was great." Even when her father sold the business and went to work for ICI she was fascinated. "I used to go down and see how things worked. I remember standing for ages watching a conveyor belt and him having to drag me away."

"Looking back on things I would like to have been an engineer. I think I would have made a good one. I don't know if I had a mathematical brain, but I certainly could have been good at it if I'd had the education for it."

The two of them fit well together as joint-managing directors of Norfrost, the simple lessons and beliefs of their childhoods retained and put to great use.

Pat fills the role of one-person marketing expert and salesforce. She is the ebullient one, with the success story constantly being retold. She retains her Teesside accent and it enhances the chunks of the commonsense advice that she dispenses to her customers. Her achievements and no-nonsense style made her Businesswoman of the Year in 1986.

Alex is very different. He is quiet and thoughtful, soft-spoken. He considers a while before producing a careful answer to questions. In an understated way he revels in his role as the engineering genius, just taking another look at the factory to see if there is anything he could dream up which would streamline and speed the production line still further.

Originally Alex capitalised on his natural bent for electronics by opening a small television shop in nearby Castletown back in 1965. He mended domestic appliances and started a thriving television-rental business. Even when they started making freezers as a full-time occupation, they kept the shop on as a useful source of cash flow, finally selling it four years ago. Having a back-up to the fledgling freezer business gave them confidence and cash-flow as well as something to fall back on if the worst came to the worst.

The shop grew and started selling general electrical goods, including fridges and freezers. The area has always made part of its living producing meat and fish, so freezers were always saleable around there well before the consumer boom.

The Grants started to wholesale freezers, but after they met someone who was making a living in Devon manufacturing 200 freezers a week they thought they should have a go themselves.

Alex, naturally innovative, thought he could just as easily make his own. True to the best stories about the genesis of small businesses, he built his first freezer in their spare bedroom. The idea of Norfrost was born.

They decided to buy two old, war-time, Nissen huts on three acres of land at Murrayfield near Castletown. With the help of David Swanson, who has been with them from the start as quality controller, they started making freezers.

For Pat the unfolding of the story is straightforward and

59

inevitable: "We started building them in ones and twos, then when we got up to ten a day we got extra people in to help us with them."

"Eventually we would make them one week and go off in the lorry and sell them the next. We had bought an old secondhand lorry for £150 and when we had to buy the next lorry, which was quite a bit more expensive, we really thought we were getting places. It really just worked from there."

The early days were simple, home-grown, hard work. The machines they bought were nearly all second-hand from bankrupt sales. "It was really hard going", Pat Grant recalls. "Sometimes we worked 48 hours without sleep just to make sure it would be possible to keep producing the freezers the next day. If a machine broke down we'd just work at it until it was working again. In those days there was no defined areas of responsibility."

"Both of us were helping on the selling, the buying, the invoicing, the engineering side or whatever. Many is the time there would be only Alec and myself left here at night putting things right for the next day."

Initially the cash for the business came from the shop. Throughout their existence they have had little help in the way of government grants. The problem throughout their early days was that it seemed such a daft place to set up a factory selling consumer goods that no one took them seriously.

Pat Grant explains: "We got very little help from any government body because they thought making white goods in the north of Scotland was impossible because it was taking the big companies all their time to make them in England, where they were presumed to know what they were doing."

"At the time there was also an awful lot of stuff coming in from Italy and places like that. They just didn't think we could compete, that we'd make a go of it. They would start by saying we hadn't any marketing expertise, and so the criticism would grow."

However, they were determined, and finally managed to get a £7,000 loan and £3,000 grant from the Highlands and Islands Development Board. "In fact it didn't buy very much in manufacturing and it hardly paid the wages for a month. It was a pretty pathetic sum but they didn't think our project was worth any more than that.''

For some years they floundered a bit: "We didn't really understand the market at the time. We started off with one model, which was an upright, and then thought perhaps we should make a wider range.'' As their later experience and success was to show, this was precisely the wrong argument. At the time it seemed sensible.

"Every year when February, March and April come round the market dies away naturally. It's a bit like trying to sell Christmas trees in January. People just don't want to know they exist. They don't think about freezers in cold weather. So you think you should be making something else.''

"So we started making another model at that time of year, on the grounds people might start buying them because they were different and we were selling them cheaply. We started making two models and that didn't go too well, so we thought that we should be making another model. We really didn't understand the marketing.''

"The other real problem was that we just didn't have enough money in the company to build up stock. In our trade you really need to be able to build up a large stock in the late winter and early spring so you can cope with the demand in the summer.''

"Either that, or you have to have the machinery and automation of plant so you can make 3,000 a week when you want them and 5,000 when you want them, just by re-setting your machines. The other alternative would be to do as some companies do and take on extra shifts in the summer, have people working from 5 o'clock until 10 o'clock or something like that.''

Pat Grant doesn't think much of companies which do that. She doesn't believe the quality can be maintained: "If you've only got people employed for three or four months of the year then you aren't building a loyalty to the company and they haven't got the experience to do it well.''

"There is a 12 week training period in most jobs before

people are properly experienced, so either you train them up and then lay them off just as they are getting good, or you train them during the day for the evening shift. But most people who want a part-time night job want it because that's the only time they can get out. Either way you are caught." The answer, as might be expected from an engineering enthusiast, is automation.

They proceeded with their battle against the market, "but we slowly came to the conclusion we made a lot of models, and no money".

2

This realization in 1977, was the turning-point. "We started slowly developing and concentrating on the one model. This was to be a small, low-cost chest freezer. We concentrated on building a market around that and letting the other models die off."

"It seemed that if we made just the one model then we could make it fast and efficiently and keep it at a price the housewife was prepared to pay, at least between £5 or £10 below anybody else."

Alex did the technical design. Pat "designed it from the housewife's point of view". "We were helped", says Alex, "by the price of food and electricity going up when Mrs Thatcher came to power. People suddenly wanted something small and cheap, just to put their weekly shopping in".

Norfrost had been making about 400 freezers a week under the old system. "Almost overnight", they jumped to 700 a week.

It was now that the perceived disadvantages of being located in such a remote part of the country were turned into advantages.

Outsiders would look at Norfrost and suggest a business like theirs should be sited on an industrial estate. The advantages, it could be argued, are overwhelming. There would be an existing infrastructure and facilities. All the services needed would be available locally. Both raw materials and finished products could be swiftly transported by existing systems.

Norfrost argue differently. The philosophy behind the isolation is expounded with feeling by Alex. It means, very simply, that "you start with no preconceived ideas about industry". That essentially means you ape no one, nor do you fall into the trap of managing a company as an end in itself. You manage the company to produce the best possible product at the best possible price.

With no facilities organised, you have to think for yourself and solve your own problems. In Norfrost's case this has led to ingenious, and eccentric, solutions that have brought admiration from its competitors.

One of these competitors, a multi-national, is reputed to have admitted it couldn't put the components into a cardboard box for the same price Norfrost sold its freezers.

If you add to this a blunt common-sense approach to buying in the few materials needed then you have a formidable combination.

Pat Grant confides: "I can actually buy a lot better than my competitors are buying. I buy in bulk and if I say I'm taking something then I take it. I take it if the market's in recession or if it's not in recession."

"I pay quickly. A lot of big companies don't. They decide the accounts side needs to take credit for three months. That means they are paying extra for it, but because they are not very good buyers they don't realise just how much extra they are paying."

"When I negotiate with someone I say, 'Right, we are going to pay you in seven days, or pay before we get it, or whatever arrangement seems best. I want terms on that. I'm going to collect it from your factory, so you've no comeback, and I want a price ex-factory. I'm taking delivery of 30,000 components because it's not worth putting our lorry in for only 2,000, I want your best price. I am not looking for a bottle of gin, or cigars at Christmas, or a free holiday in France. I am looking for the best deal for my company. I don't want any backhanders like some people do. I want a straightforward clean price for my company'. "

She combines the commonsense with a nerve and style

which produces the results they need. A good example was her notable coup over the cost of compressors.

It seemed that Japanese compressors were the best and cheapest around, but they knew they couldn't get a good commercial deal without seeing the Japanese themselves.

Pat discovered the Japanese in question were coming over to England to talk to one of their largest customers about future supplies. She persuaded the delegation to agree to see her as well if she travelled down to England. Alex spent the night endlessly taking apart and putting together a compressor for her so she would know exactly what she was talking about technically.

Then she hired an old Rolls-Royce. This meant the Japanese, already intrigued by the idea of a female managing director, would not forget Norfrost. The meeting went well and the specifications required were all negotiated. The crucial point was going to be price.

Bearing in mind the Japanese had just come from negotiating a low price with a major purchaser, Pat decided to brazen it out.

"I said I wanted the compressors at the same price, and that I knew what the price was because my father was a director of that firm, and was backing me and my husband in this small Norfrost venture."

"The fact my father had been dead for 10 years and had, in any case, worked for ICI was neither here nor there." She got her price.

The other key to their success is the accent on self-sufficiency combined with engineering ingenuity.

They produce a product which is very cheap and undercuts the market. This is mostly possible because the only parts of the freezers which are not made on-site are the motor and the thermostat. Norfrost even makes the polystyrene packaging for the final product.

In some ways the factory is a schoolboy's dream, a production line of freezers shunting through a series of systems, some highly sophisticated, some positively Heath Robinson, with the final product disappearing from view onto the back of a lorry. Yet all these processes are cutting away at costs, making basic components at costs which make the catalogue prices elsewhere look very silly.

The important point is that it is derived from the solid notion that this approach, above all, just makes sense.

If your suppliers are miles away you cannot afford to have a production line come to a halt because of a delay in deliveries. Nor, if you are Alex Grant, can you bear not to beaver away until you have found a way of making the parts yourself.

He will ask you with pride whether you have ever come across a managing director who's tool kit in his office is almost as big as his desk. His commonsense is taken as obvious: "I'm a simple Caithness boy", he says, "and I can't stand nonsense." When you talk to him of all the innovations he has made he tends to describe them modestly as 'simple technology, just simple high technology'.

All the electronics in the paint shop were designed by him: "We've had a robot in there for years", Alex confirms happily. "The union chap asked if it was reliable so I just told him, 'well it turns up every Monday morning'."

In all his endeavours in this area Alex adopts what he likes to call "the Japanese trick". Put very simply this means "you see how other people do something, then take the best ideas and do them yourself".

So instead of buying handles ready made at 50 pence a unit Norfrost has an injection moulding machine which churns them out for 10 pence a unit. The same goes for everything from the castors and hinges to the baskets inside the freezer. Over 20% of a freezer is made of plastic and Norfrost makes the lot.

Lorries which head south with a load of freezers return with 20 tonnes of polystyrene granules as their load. In the old days, when they had just started, the lorries would come back with loads of fertiliser from England for the local farmers. The principle has always been to never waste an opportunity.

This is borne out by the current loads of granules. One load of granules makes around 20,000 components. Yet if they were buying the components in and transporting them north, "we probably wouldn't get the needs of one week's production on one of our lorries''.

"We're not paying anyone else's overheads", Pat Grant points out. "We're not adding anything on to these components' costs. Whereas if we were buying them in, people would be saying 'raw materials 30 pence, on top of that I've got to pay my overheads and wages. That's another 30 pence.' In the end you probably couldn't buy it for less than 70 pence. You can say that it's always going to be at least double the raw material cost.''

The same story is true throughout their business: "If you buy in your tubing ready-bent you pay say £1.40 a unit", calculates Alex. "If you buy it unbent, and do it yourself, it costs 70 pence a unit".

Neither he nor Pat can abide the attitudes of so many middle managers elsewhere. In particular, they criticise the attitude of some companies run by managers who will buy in anything for a quiet life — it doesn't matter if it adds £1 a unit to their costs.

"We had this chap in trying to sell us pre-painted steel", Alex recalls. "But there's no way we can justify the cost, so we paint it ourselves." Norfrost could take the easy way out just as well, but would lose its competitive edge by doing so.

Part of this attitude was forced on them in the early days. The freezer market is very largely dominated by major firms. They can easily justify the sort of machinery which will maintain a massive production run. Norfrost were not in the same league.

Pat explains: "You have to remember there weren't a lot of places in Britain, or on the Continent, making small amounts of freezers like we were. Most machines we could buy would have been like using sledge hammers to crack nuts. We weren't at the capacity where we could go out in the market and buy a machine.''

"There was no point in us paying £100,000 for a machine, especially when we didn't have the money to buy a machine which was meant to do 100 cabinets an hour when we were only talking about 10 an hour. So we were forced into the situation of either having to buy second-hand machinery, which we could get quite cheaply and use for only a few hours a day, or make our own machinery if it wasn't available.''

By 1978 they had completely stopped making the range of freezers which they had once believed would make their fortune, and their full concentration was focused on one model.

''We were starting to get our costings right down on it, so we could reduce the price further, and the market took off from there. We were filling a gap in the market which hadn't been filled before at the right price. It's like a small fridge or a small cooker, something people want as a secondary thing for a family or weekend flat, a caravan or whatever. There's only a certain amount that they're prepared to pay for that type of thing. Our basic small chest freezer sells in the shops for between £79 and £89 and it will cost about £100 to fill it.''

''You have to remember a freezer is two investments. You've got to buy it and you've got to fill it, because unless you do it's going to cost you a lot of money to run it.''

3

Norfrost expanded because of their determination rather than any particular assistance they received. Using their own lorries was important to them because it meant they controlled all their distribution. They helped to keep down costs by ensuring the empty ones came north again with a paying load, even if it was only supplies for the local farmers.

Originally they relied on second-hand lorries but, in Alex's words, ''they learned me a lot of tricks that weren't worth having''. So a fleet of Scania trucks was gradually built up to supercede them.

They went back to the Highlands and Islands Development Board in 1977 for further money. This was when they were trying to fund what they felt was their major expansion scheme.

''They responded by offering us a package deal'', recalls Pat. The idea was that the Board would buy the factory from them for £40,000, ''despite the fact that it had been valued for our accounts, by the local valuer, at £59,000. They also wanted £10,000 of shares, which at that time meant 17% of the business.'' In return the Board gave them a £60,000 loan and £30,000 of grant. It meant that Norfrost got the plant and machinery it needed. However, it left a feeling of resentment behind.

''Not only were they pathetically slow in getting the money to us'', but what the Grants consider 'a dreadful conservatism' also rankles.

''The Development Board is too frightened of being taken for a ride'', says Alex. ''They will always invest in factories on the grounds that, if they are taken for a ride, they can always rent them to somebody else. However, they are very wary of helping you with working capital, which is much more useful.''

They also resented the equity stake which was put to them as an essential part of the package: ''We needed the plant and machinery and we had to take the whole package'', Pat recalls. ''It was the whole deal or none at all.''

Consequently, the Grants went back to the Board as soon as they could and bought the whole lot back off them to ensure they retained their independence and pride. That was five years later, and it cost £50,000 to get the shares back and two payments totalling somewhere around £80,000 to repurchase the factory. ''And there was a property recession on at the time'', says Pat. ''I couldn't understand that. Everywhere around us industrial property was falling down and people were taking their roofs off to avoid paying rates.''

Since the fortunes of Norfrost have improved the Board has been easier to get on with. ''They are certainly more sympathetic towards us now than then'', says Pat. A current special grant of £250,000 towards redevelopment goes some way to proving that.

The whole subject of grant policy remains a very sore point. ''If you're making profits and you get a special grant you are effectively giving half of it back to the taxman anyway'', Pat complains. She then launches into a diatribe about the inconsistencies of the grant system.

Norfrost's latest grant was to create some 50 jobs to add to the 120 they already have on the workforce. The Grants are happy with that. Norfrost is a company which has struggled and succeeded in an area of high unemployment. What they can't understand is how highly profitable American companies come over to Scotland and get huge subsidies and grants. As straightforward people, they just cannot comprehend that, when they relate it to their own experience.

"In the future we will be expanding towards 200 jobs. We export a third of our production, we buy 97% of our supplies in Britain, and no one else in this country makes a product like ours. If anyone bought another brand it would be coming from abroad", says Pat.

She warms to her theme and tells a story of another freezer manufacturer which developed into the micro-wave oven market. The factory concerned was just outside the grant area, so no money was forthcoming. "Then Zanussi wanted to build a micro-wave plant just down the road. They got government grants to do it; for training the labour, the factory, rates and rent, holidays for so many years and all the rest. Yet the British company had to compete against this sort of advantage in the market."

"Manufacturers should be looked at without taking any notice of where they are based. That shouldn't make any difference to the help available. Moreover, grants shouldn't go to companies like Nissan, who have got plenty of money to develop their businesses themselves. I think it is wrong."

She is also adamant about the stupidity of successive governments' taxation policies. She would like to see some continuity of policy. Pat cites the example of the Labour government's decision to classify electrical appliances as luxury goods: "For some stupid reason the Government dreamed up, you couldn't buy an electric iron without paying 25% VAT because it was supposed to be a luxury. Whereas you could go out and buy cocktail cabinets with only 8% VAT on them because they were supposedly not luxuries."

"I cannot understand that sort of thinking. If we decide today that we are going to spend £5 million on a five-year project, it would be a lot of money for a small business like ours. Yet the Government could come along in a year or two's time and say 'white goods are a luxury again'. You can't have a system where one minute it's worth investing £5 million and next minute it's not worth investing £5,000.''

In contrast, Norfrost have particular praise for their bankers. The Grants convinced the Royal Bank of Scotland early on that they had the drive to overcome any of the difficulties which other sources of finance had worried about. And the bank was also going to take a brighter view through its understanding of the original television rental business which provided financial security in the early days. ''With that at least we had proved we could handle money, profits and people'', says Alec.

Pat Grant is as enthusiastic about the bank as she is derogatory about Government agencies. She begins to sound like a testimonial in an advertisement: ''The Royal Bank has always been very helpful towards us and I would recommend anybody starting an industrial project to go to the Royal Bank every time.'' Norfrost investigated all the available banks at the start of their venture to see who would provide helpful backing and an understanding overdraft. ''Only the Royal Bank backed us to the hilt. They were better than any Government agency or anything.''

To convince the banks they brought in their auditors to put the figures together as a presentation: ''We'd write all the figures out and they'd put it in accountant's jargon. The way we might say it would be perfectly correct but the accountant would then express it in a way more acceptable to the bank.'' They are happy with this distinction. They have a bright young accountant doing all the in-house work and they leave it to him to translate what they know into formal information.

''We've got the feel of the company'', explains Pat. ''We know we can walk round it and know if any section is not quite as efficient as it should be. We know if we are letting things starve a little bit now, we know if a little bit of inefficiency has grown up because one part of the company has been automated and another hasn't. We know these things by running the business.''

''We're not sitting back in an office ignoring it all so that parts become inefficient. We do keep an eye on everything and know all our figures. I have an alphabetical list in my head, like telephone numbers, of the costings but at the end of the day all we care about is total wages to total production.''

The figures are worth remembering. For the year ending May 1981, Norfrost's turnover was £1,562,000 with pre-tax profits of £234,000.

By 1982 turnover had climbed to £2,517,000 with pre-tax profits of £464,090. In the year ending in 1983 the turnover had surged to £3,500,000 with pre-tax profits growing more slowly at £516,622.

4

Norfrost was maintaining its growth but obviously having a bit of a struggle with both the expenses of that growth and profitability.

''It's very hard work expanding'', Pat Grant comments, ''because you haven't got the expertise up here to expand for you. Everything's left to us to do and it's really hard work.'' Their problem is compounded by their tendency to do it all themselves anyway.

''I don't have any salesmen on the road, there's only me doing all the sales. I'm the only one doing all the buying and looking after the personnel in the factory.'' The reasoning behind this is simply one of trying to keep the overheads down. ''Every salesman is going to be at least £20,000 a year on the company's bill. If we had half a dozen of them going round the world we'd probably need another £10,000 to keep them in expenses. That wouldn't be very economical either.''

Other difficulties included the problem of convincing the workforce in the early days that Norfrost could be seen as a long-term activity. They tended to get people coming along on the grounds that it was likely to be a short-term job, and if anything else came along, then it would be wise to move.

Another problem was the shortage of sufficient money to feel they could comfortably do enough to achieve their overall goals. Again it was the problem of convincing people that Norfrost was going to be there in six years time. That didn't only apply to sources of finance. It was vital, with a consumer product, to convince the people to whom they were supplying freezers that the back-up, in terms of spares and maintenance, would be there long-term.

The only real point they had in their favour was their determination that if they wanted to do it, then the business would prosper and grow. "We just had faith in what we were doing", says Pat. They never believed, even in their worst moments, that they would go under.

"There were times when everybody else probably thought we were going out of business. We never did. There were times when it was hard going and there were times when people were saying 'you can't keep going on like this', but we just said that yes we could."

"If you're running a race you can't have people stopping you half way through. You've got to go on and they've got to let you."

Nor did they get depressed when they were up against a barrage of advice to give up: "We didn't take any notice because we knew they were wrong", retorts Pat. In part, this was because when you are completely caught up in a business there is little time to think what other people are saying. This can be disastrous in business strategy terms, but in some cases it works.

"We didn't really have the time to sit and listen to them. They'd come on the phone and say, 'Do you realise this?' We'd say 'Yes, we know that, but we haven't got time to talk now, I'm on the factory floor and I've got a visitor', and we'd put the phone down. In many ways it was a good thing we didn't really have the time to listen because we were too busy working and trying to make the company successful."

The big breakthrough, as far as sales was concerned, came when they won an order to provide freezers through the Electricity Board showrooms. Once again it was achieved through a combination of determination as well as logic taken to the lengths of eccentricity.

"It took us about six years to really get that breakthrough", recalls Pat. "I started approaching electricity boards, writing to them all and never getting any replies. I was writing very polite letters and getting nowhere. So eventually I wrote a very nasty letter to them all.''

"I said we were all forced to buy their electricity, but whenever we went into their shops all they ever had there were foreign products. Moreover they hadn't even the courtesy to reply to a British company.''

"I got about 20 phone calls and 20 letters that same week, all from the electricity boards. They told me I was going the wrong way about things, which was fine as far as I was concerned because at least I got a reaction.'' She wrote to them all again pointing out the next exhibition at which Norfrost would be showing its products.

"Eventually one of the electricity board's representatives came on the stand. He said he was looking for a frustrated 90-year-old spinster who'd been writing him nasty letters. However, they were the first electricity board to buy from us, and they are still buying from us, and we have a great relationship with them. You wouldn't expect it from a nationalised industry but on the buying side, at least, they work like a private company.''

In 1983 Norfrost won the Industrial Achievement award. Suddenly they were gaining the recognition and reward they had deserved. Television news coverage revealed not only a thriving and lively company in the far-north of Scotland, but also Pat Grant, in leotard, leading the workforce through an intensive keep-fit break.

The then Secretary of State for Industry, Norman Tebbit, when presenting the award at the Guildhall, added another personal touch to the business. He told his audience that as he prepared his speech there was something nagging away at the back of his memory. Infuriatingly he couldn't put a finger on precisely what it was. On the morning of the presentation he realised the connection.

His wife had bought a small freezer recently, and had given him the guarantee slip to send back to the company concerned. The name on that guarantee slip was Norfrost.

So the Grants not only received the cheque for winning the award, but also the testimonial of a distinguished and satisfied customer.

Part of the success for maintaining close relations with satisfied customers comes from the way the workforce at Castletown is motivated. There is a direct connection between the down-to-earth approach of the Grants and the quality of the finished product.

In the factory, where most of the jobs are fairly repetitive production-line duties, people do dull tasks with great speed and dexterity. To Pat Grant this is inevitable. To her it is similar to the way a housewife makes a bed, something which is done every day and done incredibly fast.

"Motivation comes from making people feel part of the team. You have to say to people that although they are working on the factory floor and it's a repetitive job, all jobs in this company are repetitive and not necessarily fun."

"Let's be honest. Because I'm having to speak to customers, be polite, dressed up and giving them meals, it doesn't mean to say I don't feel that I want to get on with something else. You have to understand that every job has its repetitive side."

Pat feels one of her most vital jobs is to maintain the feeling that they are all of equal importance within the company. "Making the tea in the canteen is just as important as selling freezers. All the company's tasks go towards ensuring we all avoid having to look for a job somewhere. There is nothing more boring than being on the dole, is there?"

The Grants also run a number of productivity deals. For every freezer which gets through its quality checks there is a penny for each member of staff. At the moment this gives employees an additional £30 a week on top of what is already an above-average wage for the area. Along with this comes free transport and meals, and six weeks holiday per year. When Norfrost won the Industrial Achievement award, part of the cash prize went towards an extra week's wages for everyone.

In 1984 turnover grew steadily to £3,971,000, increasing to £4,596,000 in 1985. The only fly in the ointment was that while the pre-tax profit for 1984 was up to £647,235 in 1985 it more than halved, tumbling to £288,529.

Part of that can be attributed to an attempt by the Grants to sort out their pension plans. The great majority of it was expansion ahead of profitability.

With production now averaging 3,000 freezers a week Norfrost has more or less sewn up the British market for their product. Now they are trying much harder to expand abroad, which includes providing slightly modified versions of the basic freezer for specialised export fields.

The core of Norfrost's British markets lies in providing freezers with the shops own label on them and this system is being continued abroad. They supply big freezer companies in Denmark and France in the same way they supply Bejam, Currys and the electricity boards in the UK. A different plastic label is stuck on the front, and as far as the public is concerned the freezer is no longer Norfrost but a big high-street distributors' own house-brand.

This can provide an insight into the ways the consumers' minds are believed to work. For a company which stresses the British content so hard, they still manage to stick brands' labels like Matsui on their freezers for Currys to sell in the high-street. The label still says 'Made in the UK' beneath, but the product is reckoned to sell faster with a Japanese sounding name on its front.

"We are adapting the freezers to make them tropicalised for hot countries as well. At the moment we are making one which works as either a fridge or a freezer. For example, in Pakistan. When they can get meat in bulk they can use it as a freezer, when they can't they just turn the knob and make it into a fridge", outlines Pat.

They are finding other markets in the tropics: "We have been asked to look at the idea of making them work in Land Rovers carrying medicines in Africa." Norfrost also makes versions to run off batteries for use in boats or caravans as well as adapted versions for countries where they can't get power on a constant basis. "So although we have only the one model, we do make about five versions of that particular model".

They also have plans for substantial expansion so they can cope more easily with demand. However, the estimated £4 million costs of the next five years would probably be beyond their capacity with the only help coming from the bank and future profits. Government help is being looked at, but regional development grants were stopped in the Thurso area of Caithness in November 1985. Not because the area was thriving, but because one employer was thriving — the Dounreay nuclear power station just down the coast.

"We just hope the Government's future plans for the area do not include making the whole county dependent on the one industry", says Pat drily.

5

An alternative strategy was to float Norfrost on the Unlisted Securities Market. When the Grants won the Industrial Achievement award they investigated the idea in detail. "It would be obvious for us to do it", Pat thinks. Yet once again they found they could not be satisfactorily categorised to fit into a recognisable box for sale to the market. The idea came to nothing, largely because the Grants felt the amount of cash they would raise would not be enough to justify the amount of the business which would be sold to shareholders.

Along with many famous names from recent listings, Pat Grant has done well in the various awards designed to encourage and recognise the achievements of women in business. First, she won the Business Woman's Enterprise award where, coincidentally, she was joined in the finals by Rita Battersby of VDU Installations. Then in 1985 she was a finalist in the Veuve Clicquot Business Woman of the Year award. In 1986 she won it.

She reckons she is better than most and has a business that is, as far as she is concerned, a real business. She is scathing about many of the companies which have gained great publicity in recent years through a listing on the USM and suspicious of the hype involved.

"I can't understand it when companies in the leisure markets seem to be able to raise millions when they have no real assets in the sense that we have."

"We've got a factory here with buildings that we own, 30

acres of land, plant and machinery. Solid assets that people can see. If the freezer market for some reason suddenly went dead overnight we would be a potential sheet metal basher. If you have the machinery for sheet metal you can make micro-wave ovens, cookers, fridges, anything you think you can compete with and sell. There is still something that you can do with your assets, your expertise and your labour-force.''

''Yet with some of these businesses, which are seen as tremendous successes, what do you have left if the fad on which they are built passes? You would just have empty church halls and a pile of leotards.''

To Pat this seems plain daft. She doesn't see what people are getting for their money.

Apart from the assets of the company, Pat feels that what she and Alex have is not much different from any other husband-and-wife business, except that they've been in the fortunate position to put it all into practice.

''I was fortunate in meeting my husband who's an engineer. I was fortunate that we made a good team together. I don't think either one of us could have done it alone, or without the particular background of this company. We had to come through all that to reach the depth of experience we have now.''

''When you start a company it's a bit like a young couple getting married. You'd like to buy a nice house and have it all carpeted and furnished. But if you don't have the money you can't do it, you just have to grow in stages.''

''Sometimes this is very hard for people and unions to understand. They might say, 'Well, if you can't pay the right wages then don't bother starting up, don't bother employing people'. If that was true there would be an awful lot fewer businesses, an awful lot of people would be worse off. Without the experience of starting up a business you have a different view of the business world. I think that is what is wrong with so many big companies, they could go out and put £10 million into a project and make it work for a while, but without good marketing and management experience it will fail in the end. It is just that its failure will have been disguised by its size.

We've come through it all spending our own money and having to work non-stop.''

The husband-and-wife aspect of their success is obviously very important. They fit together well, yet manage to be their own separate people at work. They tend to go their own way there. Alex to ensure that the engineering side is working to his satisfaction, while Pat takes care the customers are not just getting what they need, but are also being told what the company can do for them. ''When we get home at night we'll discuss a certain amount of it, but either we go back into work or I take a couple of keep-fit classes. It works out at perhaps only one night a week when we actually meet up and discuss things'', says Pat.

''It's a pity in some ways that we tend to take work home with us. It's probably about 10 at night before we meet up and sit down and discuss things, and then we'll still be discussing at 1 o'clock in the morning, and you can't get to sleep. We do make these pacts every so often that we're not going to discuss anything after 9 at night, but it never works.''

The standing joke is that their annual holiday consists of going round compressor factories just seeing how other people are doing it. They don't deny this, though Alex mitigates it, ''you do see a bit of the outside world when you are walking between the factories''.

However, that is just the way he is: ''I do like going and seeing engineering things. I've certainly never had a flair for nature. I'm not interested in birds, wild animals or art. I like to see them and to admire them. But I wouldn't want to ever work with them.''

He also happily admits the most beautiful thing he could imagine would be ''a well-laid out factory, highly automated with machines with their own built-in brains so that they could think for themselves, and eyesight so they could see and take decisions.''

Fortunately for the eager workforce at Norfrost he also believes that automation, although the desirable end, rarely cuts a workforce as long as the company is still growing.

In their reception area there hangs one original picture. It is abstract but has a cluster of metal tubes growing out of the painted wood surface. They bought it when down in London receiving one of their awards. Alex liked it because it had some engineering content.

They work hard at their life: "We might put in 40 or 50 hours at the factory and then perhaps another 20 at home discussing it," says Pat. "But hours don't mean anything very much."

"Initially we hardly left the factory. Some nights we actually slept on the factory floor taking two hours sleep each, taking it in turns to watch the machines and make sure that they were running properly. You have to do that sort of thing to survive in industry."

"It is not", she remarks darkly, "necessary to do that sort of thing if you are in the sort of business of making pottery or taking shells from the beach, sticking tails on them and selling them as ornamental mice. The sort of thing the Government is prone to put its money into round here."

Her management style is self-taught: "There are books on management, the same as there are books on how to succeed and win, but none of it is as easy as the books make out."

"You don't have to be born with management ideas, but you have to have the right nature to be a good manager. I don't think a highly strung, temperamental or emotional person could do it. You've got to be calm and take the problems as they arise. You've got to be a bit of an actor as well, because there'll be times when people will come to you and ask if you can help them with a personal problem, when all you want to say is that you haven't time at the moment and in any case we are all paid to make freezers, not sit around talking. But you can't say any of that, you just have to sit down and sympathise."

As for the qualities that make a particular business into a success, the Grants are unsure. The fact it is a personal enterprise counts: "You're not relying on people reporting back on bits of paper. If I want to know something I get out on the factory floor and find out for myself. The factory manager might walk in and tell me what's going on but I would still go and have a look as well", explains Pat.

"In a small company you've got your finger in every pie and you know exactly what is going on. In a big company things tend to get lost. You can have people in 25 offices juggling bits of paper all day and it doesn't mean anything. It doesn't make the company more efficient."

As for advice for people trying to set up in business, they think it is very much a matter of learning from experience.

"It really is very difficult to go into manufacturing if you are inexperienced in that area, the whole success really depends on someone's determination to succeed", Pat warns.

"There were two things we definitely made a mistake over, we hired a rotten solicitor and a rotten accountant. You want a good bank, a good solicitor and a good accountant so that you can get all the paperwork and figures through quickly."

Now their ambition is to make up to 6,000 freezers a week. The world market is there, they believe, and they are sure they are capable of getting the business.

Quite how far they can grow the business with so many of the day-to-day controls in their own hands is unsure. They are enthusiasts and enthusiasts can be blind to failings. Just as Tony Martinez at Microvitec felt engineers were their own worst enemy, so the Grants could unwittingly fall victim to the same syndrome.

Whatever happens in the future, they have built up a remarkable business through a belief in themselves, engineering self-sufficiency and large doses of enthusiasm and hard work.

Alex sums it up: "There might be some clever blokes about, but it'll take a bit to beat the both of us."

FOURTH WINNER: DENFORD MACHINE TOOLS

The story of Denford Machine Tools is very different to that of the other four winners. For a start Denford, in some form or another, has been in existence since 1931. It is a classic example of the small dynastic family firm — three generations of the Denford family have been involved in the company so far.

However, the key to its place as an award winner is its spectacular metamorphosis from a traditional Yorkshire machine-tool manufacturer — slipping quietly into unnoticed bankruptcy, its employees moving onto the dole for the rest of their days — into a world leader in a new market.

What makes this all the more remarkable is that the people concerned on either side of the transformation of Denford's fortunes are the same. The location of the operation is the same, and the skills and techniques employed were those accumulated throughout their history.

The lesson here is a simple one. For all that, it is one of the hardest for an outsider to grasp. How does a company going nowhere, in a market sector in apparently inexorable decline, manage to turn itself around without resorting to the most common 'solution': loss of family control and the appointment of a chancer and his cronies in the guise of a 'company doctor'?

Denford Machine Tools found the solution. This extraordinary feat won the company the Industrial Achievement award in 1984.

1

The company is based in Brighouse, a Yorkshire town with its past entrenched in textiles and brass bands. Buildings with proud pediments emblazoned with legends like 'Perseverance Mill Erected 1851' abound. Most of them are in a poor state or being converted into shops, which sit uncomfortably in the heroic scale of the stonework. The textile businesses, which used to employ whole families in the workforce, have mostly gone. Unemployment is high. It has become a depressing place. Half of the people here are 'unemployable anyway' a local will tell you. 'They know with the dole and their wives going out to work, they will have just enough to get by on. They'll have their beer money' is the common view.

In a small industrial estate by the river Calder, Denford has its home. There is a pub on the corner and the other factory buildings on the estate are interspersed with outbreaks of 'no-man's land' where nature and old car chassis combine to form the landscape.

Denford's premises look very much the same from the outside as a million or so small factory businesses across the country. The only hint of prosperity is the chairman's Mercedes outside with numberplate DEN 4D. This, as Gerald Denford explains, is the only luxury in which they have indulged.

Gerald Dunford is a modest man with a soft Yorkshire accent, despite having been born in Chingford outside London. He makes no fuss about their success, nor does he try to baffle you with science. He is the archetypal family businessman, his satisfaction derived from the simple source of running his own business and enjoying it.

The business was started in 1931, the year Gerald was born. His father began making jigs, tools and fixtures "in the back garden" in Chingford. The company grew and, in the years before the Second World War, turned to the production of aircraft jigs, tools and fixtures. "Immediately the war started an unexploded shell landed on part of the factory and demolished it." The Ministry, eager to protect wartime production capacity, insisted they move "to somewhere in the sticks''. So the embryo Denford company came to Yorkshire, although ''part of the factory finished up in Halifax and continued working mostly for the aircraft industry''.

After the war, in which time the labour force had doubled, those seconded from London decided to return. The rest, including Denford's father, decided to stay in Yorkshire. The only problem was that he didn't think Yorkshire was the ideal place from which to service the building of aircraft. So he looked at the traditional Yorkshire industry and decided to go into machine-tools, specialising in lathes, and did so for several years.

''But through all sorts of circumstances, including ill-health, he decided to sell out and did exactly that'', recalls his son Gerald. ''He consulted me, but I wasn't much interested at the time in the machine-tool industry. I was 21 and, although an apprentice engineer working in the company, I didn't feel my particular interests were going to be with that type of industry at the time''.

He did his National Service with the air force. By the time he came out his father, having decided that working within the large group to which he had sold out was the wrong decision, had bought a Brighouse-based company making textile machinery.

As is the tradition in family businesses, his father told Gerald there were certain things he was not happy with in his new acquisition. ''He said 'would you go and sort out this and sort out that and sort out the other'. So I wound up coming down here. I sorted out the various things he wanted doing and eventually I stayed here''. The Denford story proper had got under way.

The new company did what so many other machine tool makers did; produced well-engineered tools for secure and settled markets. It was a good living and a tried and tested one. They started by making machine tool accessories for another manufacturer and progressed to making much bigger machine tools which themselves were destined to be part of larger milling machines. For 20 years, between 1957 and 1977, they sold their production in fairly large numbers to satisfied customers. They had also begun selling a specialist range of machine-tools for the education and training market. This was the key to survival when the industry collapsed.

In Gerald Denford's words, "the results of the oil crisis dropped on almost every manufacturer, the gravy train had come up against the buffers". The days when manufacturers could almost forget why they were making the stuff, and simply keep churning out the production because the orders were there, had come to an end. As it turned out, so had much of the UK machine-tool manufacturing business. The entrepreneurs of the Far East, with their ability to reassess and learn, allied with low costs, took over.

Denford's salvation lay in the fact they were already involved in a specialist area, that of making training machines. This had developed almost by accident, and dated back to his father's work. "The original Boxford lathe my father made wasn't a training machine. It was really a tool room or model-maker's machine, but it became apparent in the mid-1950's that the biggest market was selling it into the training market. We decided that if it was still successful, even though it hadn't been designed for training, then we should aim for that market specifically." This they did, and the demand was gratifying. Unwittingly, the niche was established, the groundwork laid, for Denford's metamorphosis.

However, following the oil crisis the first step Denford took was to modernise their range of machines "as best we could" to try and make them more attractive to customers. It was the strategy of going for a bigger slice of a smaller cake, with the very limited resources of a declining player. So they updated the technical specifications and tried to give them a more modern appearance. The business might be in decline, but at least they were selling products which looked as though they might be part of the future.

2

Then the crucial change was made. Like so many crucial changes it did not come about through the work of planning committees enjoined to come up with future product development nor even through a single flash of inspiration. It came through a couple of chance remarks which stuck in Gerald Denford's mind and his consequent decision there was potentially an opportunity there for the company.

Computer Numerically Controlled (CNC) machine-tools was the result. As their sales brochure now records: 'Originally with a reputation for high-quality, conventional machine-tools, Denford recognised the importance and potential capabilities of high-tech, low cost micro-processor controls. Research and development efforts were focused on control systems and, in particular, software.'

The benefit of hindsight in the sales talk makes the whole transformation seem very obvious and planned. It was not.

"We made a lathe which we called the 'Synchro'. We had some people over from Finland who saw it and suggested that if we put a CNC on it we could make a good training machine. At the time my reply was 'You must be joking. We've got quite enough problems without trying that'. Then, almost a week later, someone from the college in Hull where my son was training was here, and said 'You want to put a CNC control on that machine. It would be ideal for training'." The combination of the two remarks decided Denford. CNC was the future.

He knew from his own experience that there was a need for training. "By that time we already had several CNC machines in our plant. When they came in no one had the faintest idea how to operate them." Having taken the decision to go in that direction they also made one more crucial decision. They accepted it was a fairly sophisticated business. They also recognised that what makes it even more complex is that, with a comparatively sophisticated production machine, there are a lot of peripherals associated with its programming. You don't need to know about all that at the beginning.

Denford explains "It's like taking one of those learner-driver Mini Metros with dual controls. You neither want nor need to know about heated rear windscreens or electrically operated seats or cruise control. What you need to know are the basic controls."

Denford produced a basic CNC training lathe which they

called the Micro Master. It was designed and sold over a period of two years. They were the first in the field, but "although it was not at all clear at that time, it is perfectly clear now," it was not going to provide volume sales. Competitors realised what was happening and came into that part of the market. So Denford decided to design a bench machine from scratch and target it as a specially designed machine for the job, 'much as a London cab is'. That machine was the Orac. Since then they've gone on to design and produce another five machines which have all sold extremely well. Over 2,000 machines have been sold and they are now able to produce a big machine like the Quatromill, which they say is suitable for both light production and for advanced training. "We've got a half-way house situation there", grins Gerald Denford.

Denford's success was not achieved through a simple and straightforward recognition of the solution followed by a resolute and logical pursuit of the goal. It was, in the way of most businesses, attained almost in spite of all the avenues which are supposed to be helpful at such times. They tended to trip over their own enthusiasm. They were almost always short of cash and, at one point, they were on the verge of being closed down by the bank.

Talking to the people at Denford about this period, one gets an almost endearing sense of the chaos in which they must have worked as they sought to change completely the direction in which the company was going to have to move.

They started by working with a company of electronic engineers in Huddersfield. The object was a low cost control and after looking at what was available on the market, Denford produced its own specification. At this stage according to Gerald Denford, "we just got on and did it". But at the same time they also applied for a development grant to help out.

This was a disaster. There was no chance, whatsoever, that the grant system could manage to process its work at a speed which would keep up with Denford. They put the appropriate application in but the actual work accelerated.

"As the 1980 machine-tool exhibition was almost upon us at the time, and we knew that it would be vital, we put a spurt

Pat and Alex Grant of Norfrost

Gerald Denford of Denford Machine Tools

Gio Benedetti (centre) of Industrial Clothing services

on, working all hours, to get the damn thing finished.'' The result was ''we then got one of their inspectors coming up here, telling us they weren't in the business of allowing retrospective grants, that we would forfeit the grant thenceforward because we had accelerated our development programme''.

The grant they would have got, some 25% of £150,000, was a lot to lose for a company struggling to develop a new product. ''In the end'', as Denford now phlegmatically concludes, ''you have to go the way the wind is blowing. At that time the wind was blowing very strongly, telling us there was a market there for the product. So we lost the grant and the money had to come from other cash flow we generated.''

Denford was still selling a reduced range of their traditional products, so there was some cash coming in, and they managed to raise some money from the banks. At this point, when Gerald Denford tells the story he tends to smile a lot: ''At that time we carried on almost to the brink, probably doing all the wrong things, but it was one of those times when everything turned out all right in the end.'' He also thinks the fact everyone in the company was so euphoric about the future, managed to confuse the banks. ''No one here really doubted the whole thing would be successful in the long run. It was really a question of how far we could stretch the elastic without it breaking. When you've never been that far, you don't know how elastic it is.''

They were about to find out.

Until then, the impression they had of the banks was that there was not much in the way of informed help available for a business like theirs. Yet when they were in the greatest trouble they found it was the banks which came to their aid. Barclays in Leeds, had set up a fire-brigade department as part of the national effort by banks to be seen as trying to save businesses rather than as the agents of their collapse. Alarm bells were ringing as a result of the state of the Denford bank position and they sent someone down to investigate.

''The aim'', as far as Gerald Denford was concerned, ''was just to see that all the things that we were saying were, in his opinion, accurate. Also to check our records to make sure we hadn't got any fiddles going on with the stock or the work in progress, that kind of thing.''

"He spent a week here doing a full investigation on everything and came up with a very favourable report." As a company they had been at pains to produce full cash-flow forecasts and figures every three months for the bank, but they realised that the figures were not the whole story. "All the guy's report did was confirm everything that we had been saying.''

Dealing with banks is a hard process for many small or struggling companies.

Gerald Denford has his own ideas on how they work. Like many a small businessman, his ideas are on the cynical side: ''We probably made the mistake of giving them the exact facts and figures, which is something that a lot of people don't. We know a lot of people who go into the banks with a few notes on the back of a matchbox and they seem to get away with it. Those are the sort of people who cause the banks a lot of aggravation.''

"We have always had a company secretary who has produced facts and figures which could be scrutinised by anyone. The unfortunate thing is that when banks see figures like that, they really only look at the bottom line because they don't fully understand the business. The guy who came to do the investigation did a first class job. We didn't give him any bullshit, but we did just give him enough cream to go on top of the cake for it to be attractive enough for them to continue.''

Denford was also in the position where they knew there was not much further to go before they would know whether they had a success on their hands or not. If the bank had not decided to send an investigator down, and had instead pulled out what it was owed, the company would no longer exist.

In mid-1981 they got an order from the US for eight machines. This was the turning point. They got the machines out to the US very quickly, and almost equally crucially, managed to get paid very quickly. This was harder than it might have been. In the past Denford had had payments problems with this particular company, so they decided to opt for Yorkshire bluntness. Either they paid against a pro-forma invoice or they didn't get their machines. The US firm paid up. Denford heaved a sigh of relief. Success with the new strategy was not just theoretical, it was now a practical proposition.

3

Gerald Denford, as the chairman of a struggling company, was also suffering from the financial uncertainty. These days he smiles and holds a level hand to a point somewhere above his forehead: "I was in up to about there with no oxygen", he recalls, "houses, possessions, the lot."

"I wasn't happy about it, but I had enough confidence in what I was doing to realise we had a good chance of surviving. We were even prepared to sell off some of the land and buildings." In actual fact, they did try this. Even here the local economic conditions thwarted what, at one point, was seen as a lifeline. A local factory agreed to buy some of the Denford premises only to raise endless legal points about a right of way. The sale fell through. Unknown to Denford the other factory was suddenly having a terrible time, a legal nicety became the face-saving device to avoid the impossible purchase.

At this point Denford opened the rather grandly titled 'Theatre of Advanced Technology'. This is a section of the factory where the products are displayed in quiet surroundings, where technical colleges and other training bodies can sample the machines and the technology. Companies can also send their own staff along to be trained on machines they have bought or intend to buy. It is a classic example of how to enhance your products and make sure that the customer can see what he is buying. It took more cash than they could spare, at a time when they probably couldn't spare it, but on a simple view of how to sell their products and save themselves, it was the right decision.

Finally Denford's problems began to recede. They had the product and they were beginning to have the money. Gradually they sold the machines in larger quantities and, by generating extra cash, gained the confidence of the bank and reduced the overdraft. Larger orders followed. One of them, a bonanza from Mexico, really assured Denford of the time to put the company on the sort of footing where it could plan solid growth for the future and forget, without becoming complacent, the battle to survive.

The problems became those of selling and distribution. With a specialised niche in the market and the potential for great export revenue, this is not as simple as it might be. The overseas distributor game has been disastrous for many companies, many of them a good deal larger and more experienced than Denford. Their approach has been sensible. Denford has tried to pick a different type of distributor for each of its markets in an attempt to marry need with conditions. In the US they have a sole-distributor selling throughout who has coverage in every State. ''We are lucky to have them and they plunged into it feet first along with us. They spend a lot of money on marketing and that's working out very well.'' Having a product which is aimed at education and training people makes things easier. There are not many people aiming for the market, and the US has been happy to allow outsiders fill what is seen as a minority market.

Europe is different. In Norway they go against the US experience and sell through a machine tool distributor instead of a training specialist. They find that in a market like Norway, where there is a comparatively close-knit community, it is perfectly possible for the general distributor to get the word across to specialist customers. It does not always work so well. Elsewhere in Europe the company has found that its problems appear to be almost insuperable in getting someone to sell the product effectively.

Selling in the UK has gone well because they have kept it simple. They have what they believe to be a good product, they have done a lot of effective advertising through the technical press to the right potential customers. They also recognise that, in a specialist world, the best sort of advertising is editorial coverage in the industry's newspapers and magazines. As any good businessman will point out, this has the benefit of being free and customers take more notice of the editorial than the advertising. Denford also took the trouble, via their 'theatre' idea, of building up good relationships with technical colleges and education authorities. In a short time they had ensured their initial lead was turned into something much more substantial.

These were the easier aspects of their efforts to regain growth. The real problems which remained were all financial. Expansion, particularly when it involves substantial investment in research and development, is always hard. Currently, with a turnover of around £5 million, they are spending about £250,000 a year on developing and maintaining new products. Gerald Denford reels off a long list of areas where he feels it is of great importance to spend more of the hard-won income: "We have a very extensive demonstration facility, which doubles for training. We are extending the range of products we are selling into the CAD/CAM and flexible manufacturing systems market. We are modernising the factory step by step. We have installed new lighting. We are decorating — we have to ensure the place looks high-tech and that we keep up our appearances. We've spent £15,000 on redecorating and refurbishing the offices. We've got computerised systems in everywhere — accounts, stock, work in progress, computer aided design — the whole place is computerised from A to Z. We have got work stations all over the place." Denford strongly believes this is important. They have to convince their customers they are dealing with an efficient and advanced supplier, quite apart from making sure that they stay ahead of their competitors.

The list continues: "We have put in a separate generator system so we are independent of the Yorkshire Electricity Board. We can't afford to be shut down for hours on end through Mr Scargill or anyone else. We've got back-up facilities for compressed air, for instance, we've put in a new, low-bake painting system."

The philosophy is again that of common sense. "We are putting money in to make ourselves efficient, so that we've got some wool on our back if there's any kind of recession. The more machines we make in our range the more accessories and equipment there will be which are compatible.''

Denford's greatest success was the huge £1.5 million order which provided it with its Mexican bonanza. It transformed the pre-tax profits for 1984. Prior to that year the turnover had been growing steadily, losses were turning into good solid, though unspectacular, profits. In 1981 turnover was £1.15 million, in 1982 it grew marginally to £1.20 million, and this increased steadily to £1.67 million in 1983. In 1984 turnover leapt to £4.16 million which continued through to 1985 with a turnover of £4.69 million.

The pre-tax figures illustrate the point even more clearly. In 1981 there was a loss of £7,000. This grew to £15,000 in 1982, but by 1983 a modest profit of £20,000 was made. From there the figures rocket with the 1984 pre-tax profits coming through at £726,000. After the Mexican contract had worked its way through, the 1985 pre-tax profit fell back to a more realistic £491,000.

Useful though the Mexican contract was, the consequent distortion to the figures has been a mild irritation. Gerald Denford, a man of common sense rather than of financial rules, has his own way of looking at it.

''If you had taken the 1984 and 1985 figures together, done a proper sort out so that you could see how the business was progressing, then it would have given a better impression. We got a lot of very big orders in together and we had to work a lot of overtime to get the stuff out. On one of the orders we were talking about 250% net profit on some of the items. You are not going to get that sort of payday coming up every year. Unfortunately it all had to be through by about 15th March that year. I tried to spread it over the end of our financial year at the end of March but I couldn't. It gave us a huge boost but it did distort the figures. To maintain the turnover and actually increase it the following year was a hell of an achievement. The profits came down to what you might call a more realistic level then.''

Nevertheless the Mexican contract gave them the ballast, from a relatively simple contract, which meant relative prosperity could make a long-awaited return to the whole Denford operation. The contract was to supply 22 colleges throughout Mexico, part of an overall £35 million package spent in the UK. They were lucky with that. It meant "the money for education and training was supplied by UK banks. In the event, we need not have had Export Credit Guarantee Department cover. Everything was what it seemed to be. You find out people are honest."

On the other hand the latest of Denford's schemes to maximise the benefits of its achievements is unlikely to succeed. The idea was to build what they planned to call the 'Galaxie Teaching Centre'. This was a much bigger version of the existing 'Theatre of Advanced Technology' and one which could have been exported complete to customers abroad. It was a grandiose idea but one which might have worked. Gerald Denford enthuses: "We can sell this worldwide as a complete package deal for developing countries and, in some cases, developed countries where the infrastructure isn't complete. It means that we can assemble something here, like our demonstration facility, into a PortaKabin type package, deliver it complete to a customer in Saudi Arabia and have it running inside 24 hours." The cost was calculated to be "something like £750,000".

The oddities of the Government's support system ruled it out, quite apart from any arguments on its merits or the likelihood of its success. "There's no money available for buildings, there's no development grant available in this bloody area because we are in Calderdale, not in the Wakefield enterprise zone and so on and so on."

It is a small part of the Denford story. However, it does illustrate how even a successful businessman finds himself frustrated by a system which, he feels, promises much but rarely delivers. Forgetting the project itself, Denford's gripes are typical of many a company's experience.

"There is money available for software, associated with the development costs which would total about £250,000. We would get grants of about 25% to 30% of that. It's just not worth putting an application in with all the aggro you've got to go through. It's not worth a light. So we made a proper presentation and I've met the Minister. He was well aware of the possibilities associated with the project and said we should take it further, put a proper presentation forward. We've done that, then eventually they turn round and say there's no money for it. Occasionally there is 'special money' available, but there's none at the moment.''

"We can't fund it ourselves. It would stretch the elastic right back to where we were five years ago. We can do very nicely with what we've got. It's just a pity.''

4

Gerald Denford finds what he sees as a gulf between Government thinking and action at a local level a difficult problem for small companies trying hard, perhaps sometimes too hard, to develop their products and their market.

As a result of the awards Denford Machine Tools has won, he has done the rounds of Government receptions and conferences. He has even had his invitation to 10 Downing Street. Apart from Number 10 being "much bigger and smarter than I expected," he reckoned that at that level they had, what seemed to him, the right attitudes. They were encouraging. They seemed to understand the difficulties a growing business had to overcome, they seemed to be listening to his grumbles as well as the more positive side of his message.

It is what happens to those policies when they reach local and tangible levels that concerns Denford.

"It is surprising that the attitudes the Government officials have don't filter down through the civil service, the Department of Trade and Industry and through to a few more. I think the will is there, there is much more awareness in these areas than there ever used to be. It's just that, somehow, they can't break away from their chains. They are all pretty well tuned onto the right wavelength now, yet they can't seem to do anything about it.''

Denford is phlegmatic though and accepts that what he has to do is keep the business expanding and the company growing. The programme of widening the range continues, along with the theory that it makes a company less vulnerable to unexpected changes in the market if they have other machines as well as all their back-up parts and accessories, into which to divert their efforts.

Denford is developing into multi-language facilities to ensure they can pick up any export opportunities they spot. They also see the growth in computer aided design and manufacturing (CAD/CAM) as an obvious area to boost expansion along with the greater emphasis on flexible manufacturing techniques. "There is a wide range of advanced manufacturing techniques associated with our products which are perfect for the training area".

He also sees growth on the training side being spurred on partly by the trainees themselves. Having taken a close interest in the ones who have been to his Theatre of Advanced Technology he is happy with the future. "All the kids are computer-oriented now and are themselves asking for, pushing for, more sophisticated ways of using the equipment."

This belief in a livelier and better workforce across the whole industry extends to his own people: "When we began we only had about 15 people making textile machinery and various other bits and pieces. This gradually grew through to the late 1970's when we had about 115 people. Then with redundancies, wastage and everything else as we went down to rock bottom, we had only about 65. That was only just viable in terms of overheads and related costs. These days we have our largest staff ever with around 125 people."

Not only is it the largest, which is good for an area hard hit by unemployment, but Denford thinks it is the best.

Part of this comes from the underlying assumption in the area that unemployment is inevitable: "It is obviously a damn sight easier to motivate now than it used to be. But we also have a lot more younger employees than we had and I find that at the younger end of the spectrum, helped by the fact we are producing advanced products, they are very easy to motivate. They realise they can't go anywhere else and get a better job. Provided we give them a proper salary and reasonable incentives, like bonus schemes on production, then they are

95

very happy to work here.'' A proper salary means about 10% more than they could get elsewhere. Denford expects to get and keep the people they want. ''There's no use in having two men doing one man's job. It's better to have one man with greater incentives in front of him.''

''Like any organisation, it's all about the people who are employed in the company. If you haven't got the right people and a proper selection method for employing the right people, then it's extremely difficult to make progress. It will always be three steps forward and three steps back if you are not careful.''

Gerald Denford attributes part of the difficulties for industry in general, and Denford Machine Tools in particular, in the past to the problem of holding not just a stable workforce but one that consisted of the key people they needed.

''Part of the historical development of this company was choked by the lack of an efficient labour force in the late 60's and early 70's because we just couldn't get the right people.''

''Now we're able to be more selective in the type of people we employ and we can get a very, very good team together. It is an unfortunate reflection on things that you only arrive at that situation when you've got, in this case, three million unemployed.''

''You had immense problems when people were being bought and sold literally across the street. Companies just kept offering 20% extra in salary and people moved across. Inevitably the same process had to hold good for your recruitment as well. All it really did was jack up salaries and inflation and eventually put three million out of work. Running a business is all about organisation and motivation, if there isn't a profitability factor in the middle then you're lost.''

Motivation also brings in the whole area of taxation. This is another topic which the ordinary small businessman traditionally finds baffling. It is not that the techniques or organisation of taxation are confusing, though that can sometimes be the case. More often the policy itself fails to make much sense when one is seated in a factory rather than in the Treasury or Somerset House.

For Gerald Denford collecting tax from earnings seems plain daft: "I have always thought the best method of taxation was at the source of purchase. The Pay-As-You-Earn system in this country has a lot to answer for when you are looking at lack of incentive for the labour force."

He argues income tax should be eliminated for anyone earning less than, say £12,000. The tax needed to make up the deficit this would produce should be raised by a sales tax, probably in the form of an increase in VAT.

"Men on the shopfloor, whether they earn £100 a week or £200 a week, want to have that amount in their pockets so it is their decision how to spend it." Again Denford feels this is a message the Conservative government under Margaret Thatcher has preached, but not put into practice.

He is also critical of tax incentives on the corporate side which, he feels, can encourage companies to make erroneous decisions. He is happy the old idea of capital allowances for plant and machinery has been phased out: "Much better that it all be down to depreciation in the future", he argues. "There were so many people attracted to buying all kinds of wrong equipment. They were dashing in to get something bought by the year-end, the only result was that they bought the wrong equipment for the wrong reasons and at the wrong time."

5

Denford's recent successes, after such a bleak period, have brought it more than its fair share of awards. Apart from the Industrial Achievement award in 1984, it has added several others. Enough to fill a cramped reception area with impressive certificates to inspire confidence in visitors and buyers.

They won the export award for small businesses for 1984-85. Sponsored by British Caledonian, Midland Bank, the British Overseas Trade Board and Thomas Cook, the award opened further doors in the export world. Gerald Denford is much more relaxed about exports than most small businessmen. In fact he declares that payment from people abroad is better and more reliable than from customers in the UK. This partly stems from Denford's blunt approach to the problems of the export market: "If they supply a letter of credit, drawn on a UK bank, we sell to them. If they can't, then we don't."

The company has also won awards for its technology. It became one of the three finalists in the British Micro-Computing Awards in 1985. Sponsored by the Barclays Bank high technology team, this was for the best micro-computing application in an established industry — a category which might have been invented with Denford Machine Tools in mind.

Gerald Denford is modest about their success in the award-winning field: "For one thing, we have filled in the application forms and other people don't. Also, we have a range of products which are quite startling in their own sphere. That's all." The result has been prestige, a much wider public awareness of Denford's activities and a good feeling of recognition and stability which encourages both customers and suppliers.

When one company spots a new market and becomes a recognised success in that market, it generally means something else as well — tough competition ahead. Denford views the invasion of his patch as something which should be welcomed.

"We keep adding to the facilities available on each machine. By upgrading them all the time we would hope to keep ahead of the competition. There is a lot of competition now, worldwide. People have seen that we've been successful. In many ways each company rides on the back of the success of other companies. But we don't object to competition."

"In fact it quite often accelerates our own development programme on products. It can also act as a guideline for our own product development because sometimes we can't see our way forward and we learn from them. We will make our own judgements but it is always very useful to know what our competitors are doing as well."

An obvious next step might be towards a place on the Unlisted Securities Market. Denford's argument against such a move is that they are a family business and keen to keep it that way. "I've got my son in the business as technical director and my daughter is business systems manager. I get a good living out of it and so do they."

Going on to the USM is seen rather in the light of something other companies do when they have one or two profitable years behind them and the owners want to cash it in. At Denford the family connections argue towards building a company with a product line with a long-term future.

The same argument extends to the idea of either selling-out or buying another company to aid expansion. "Having seen what has happened elsewhere to companies which have sold out, I have no wish to get into that situation," Denford states categorically. The answer to the question of making an acquisition is equally simple: "Why take on someone else's problems?"

Denford is overwhelmingly family-owned, but both the works director and the company secretary have been with the company through much of its history of trials, tribulation and success and "are well entrenched in the company in terms of involvement and shares". Denford points out, "they might just as well be family for the amount of time and involvement they put into the company".

They are happier with that arrangement: "We are all working for ourselves. We don't want to be working for a bunch of shareholders who are outside the company. I really have no particular interest in the USM at all. I work about 10 hours a day and if I'm away on exhibitions I work longer hours. In certain circumstances I work less. We do what we consider necessary to run the company efficiently."

6

In many ways the whole small-business climate in recent years has moved against the family business tradition. The target now tends to be a USM listing as soon as possible. While this does not stop family businesses being formed, and continuing as family businesses, it focuses attention on the idea of running a business along the lines of a public company. This means the localised family business which is intended to provide a living for a wide range of people in a particular area, as well as enriching its founder and those members of the family who prove capable of carrying it on, has rather faded as an ambition.

Gerald Denford thinks there is not much difference in the basic ideas which provide success: "It's a question of properly defining the markets you are going to be involved in, then making sure you are making enough money in the sector of the market into which you are selling to generate enough cash to make it all worthwhile."

"That is precisely what we didn't do for so long, until we got ourselves involved in the product range we have now. It's very easy to look at sales and not look at the bottom line. It doesn't matter what business you are in, whether it's ice-creams, machine-tools or matches and bootlaces on the street corner, it's the bottom line that matters."

"You've also got to make sure you don't part with it all too quickly either. So many people associated with family businesses in the past have taken everything out and put nothing in. That particularly applies to the Yorkshire woollen industry."

"At Denford we take, comparatively speaking, very little out of the company. It is our aim to make it self-generative so that the assets are within the company. Providing those assets are the right ones, they should then generate more assets."

Gerald Denford is convinced the company will continue to prosper and believes that much of the work they have done in past years will start coming through in the form of greater profitability in the future. He sees himself as a 'jack-of-all-trades' and tells tales of how he used to shift the coke from the front entrance round to the boilerhouse in the early days.

He likes the fact there is a human scale to what he makes: "You can relate very easily to the product. It's not like some machine tools these days, when they're getting to being the size of a room. When you get to that stage, then they start becoming a bit distant. You can't actually see or feel much of what they're doing nowadays. You shut the guards, press a button, there's a shower of sparks and chippings, next minute the finished part comes out. Whereas on our products you can see exactly what you are doing."

His sense of realism also extends to his own skills within the business: "I consider myself to be able to do most things, nothing very well, but most things adequately", he sums up.

His views on the prospects for the company are equally solid and sensible: "We will see relatively small increases in actual turnover, but as time goes by we will find the business is more and more profitable as a result of the amount of research and development we have put into the company. With that amount of effort, we should have put the company onto a firm, concrete base. Whereas in the past a lot of the results have not come from a firm base. They've come from one with a few loose rocks around."

"We were lucky with a few of the orders we got in the past and will build on that, but in the future we need to have a multiplicity of orders from all kinds of situations and countries."

"Much of the groundwork has now been done. We have done a great deal of work on all kinds of markets where there are not many machines now being sold. Those will all blossom".

Gerald Denford has, one can argue, been lucky. However, the real reason why he is still there is that he didn't give up when many other people were doing so. No one would have backed a small Yorkshire-based machine-tool maker in the midst of a massive recession in both his own narrow sector and the world economy.

Fortunately, adopted Yorkshireman that he is, he looked patiently to see where his chances of survival lay. When he saw the answer, immediately he set about ensuring his company put all its effort and determination into winning its fight for success.

FIFTH WINNER: INDUSTRIAL CLOTHING SERVICES

Since its great days of industrial supremacy the west coast of Scotland has been in sorry decline. The great shipbuilding and heavy engineering businesses still exist, but only as a ghostly presence by comparison with the earlier, vigorous, days of prosperity.

While the imposing Victorian office buildings of Glasgow may seem to be on a different scale to their present occupants, there has been a movement on the west coast which has been creating businesses steadily throughout that period of decline. It has created a network which now stretches far beyond the area. It all stemmed from one cafe in the seaside town of Largs.

This is Nardinis. Since the 1890's it has not just been the mecca for sweet-toothed Glasgow schoolboys, but also the unofficial business school of countless Italian immigrants to Scotland. They have arrived with their suitcases, a recommendation from an uncle and little else, but after a few years have moved on to start their own businesses. Nor have these just been thousands of ice-cream vendors and cafe-owners. They have gone from these beginnings to more than corner-shop enterprises. Trusthouse Forte is perhaps the greatest success story that the system can boast. Fresh examples are still emerging.

The latest is Industrial Clothing Services. Run by the noisy but genial Gio Benedetti, it is based in Irvine in Ayrshire and won the Industrial Achievement award in 1985.

1

Benedetti's achievement was to change a straightforward high-street dry-cleaning business into an industrial cleaning business which took on work which no one else had thought of touching. Instead of the British motor industry treating the protective gloves it uses in their thousands as disposable, it now has them cleaned and repaired by Benedetti's company. Ford alone saves over £1 million a year as a result.

It all seems terribly obvious now. At the time no one had seen the potential, the huge business it could become. Hindsight, as with many winners of the award, makes the initial idea seem very simple. The rare ability to turn that idea into business reality is the result of both character and personality. Gio Benedetti has great resources of both.

Benedetti's success stems from an innate stubbornness fed by an aggression that tells him not only is his way right, but there is no reason why he can't achieve his immediate and long-term goals. He is large, genial and generous. By listening to his accent one can work out from where his qualities come.

As he speaks there are two competing cultures tumbling out in his conversation. At times the Italian accent is uppermost; expansive and wordy. Then in mid-sentence the gruff, clipped and sparing Scots comes roaring back. It is no wonder he has been so successful in convincing customers to use his company's services.

Benedetti left Italy when he was 11 years old. His father worked in a large chemical factory and they lived in a small village sixty miles from Florence. He recalls boyhood days as being simple, sunny times.

"We lived well, we had our own house and a nice garden. All we kids met up by the river every day. All I remember is sunshine. It was only a wee village with one telephone and two cars."

They already had relations in Scotland. Two uncles were running a cafe in Ayrshire. "They would come from Scotland with their new car and that would be the only time I'd been in a car."

For a small boy in a small village it meant only one thing:

"The impression was that it was all happening in the outside world."

Gio had been quite bright at school but he had finished his elementary education. In Italy, the next phase had to be paid for, so his uncle's offer to take him over to Scotland to learn English was attractive: "It turned out to be Scottish English that I learned, but it was obviously a big decision for my parents. They said OK we'll send him over for a year or so."

He doesn't remember the day he left, but the last time he was back an old woman who did remember told him "the whole village was out waving bye-bye at the station. There was me with my wee case not giving a damn. I didn't know what I was going to."

His uncle had a cafe in Irvine, Ayrshire, and the idea was ostensibly to do some work in the cafe and go to school as well. He soon found out it was the cafe work that was the main reason for his visit to Scotland: "The idea of school was only a cover by my uncle. I was working from 8 am to 11 pm with school in between and never a day off. The only relaxation was if I could steal a half an hour during my lunch break to go to the swings or something."

It was tough at school as well. Arriving in a Scottish school at that age, without speaking much of the language, was not the easiest way to survive: "When I started at school I couldn't speak any English. I was eleven years old and stuck in primary five playing with plasticine. I just sat there."

"You've got a school with maybe a thousand kids and there's you from Italy. They all look at you as though you've come from Mars. In the playground they would all gather round, looking at you and prodding you to get you to move or say something, anything. So the first words I learned were 'fuck off'."

The whole period was obviously a very unhappy one, but the young Gio survived. He now says that the experience of school and the cafe were good training: "You ended up in a few arguments but you learned to stand up for yourself. And if you got one day off work at the cafe you thought you were in paradise."

It also provided him with the contacts he would need later on. His doctor, his accountant and his lawyer were all in the same class with him at school. His sales director is an old schoolmate as well.

He left school at 18 and found himself working full-time at the cafe: "I hated it and detested it. Tea, coffee, sugar and milk. That was the extent of taxing my brain. It was something to do but that was as far as it went."

The young Benedetti was told by his uncle that the cafe would be his — when the uncle retired in some twenty years time: "I didn't cherish that idea", he recalls, with almost English understatement.

By the time he was 21 he had saved £200 and he decided the answer was to open a small local business which would be his to run in his own way: "I looked in the local paper and saw a dry-cleaning business for sale in Kilwinning. I knew nothing about dry-cleaning but I thought 'let's have a look at it'. "

The owner wanted £1,500 for the business. Benedetti encountered his first hostile bank manager: "The deal was that, with my couple of hundred, I would need £500 from the bank and the owner was happy to take the balance over a two-year period with some interest. The bank said I was too young to ask for £500, which was a lot of money in those days. Its equivalent now would be around £5,000."

Even then, he was a stubborn and persistent character and he finally convinced the bank. He bought the whole business: "The building, the plant and machinery, a van and everything else. The business employed four people and I knew nothing about it." There were problems from the very start.

"I was a bit naive. What I didn't realise when I bought it was that the guy had been running it down, that it had already lost a lot of its business to others. Add to that the fact I knew nothing about dry-cleaning. The guy had told me not to worry because he would stay on for two months and teach me all I needed to know. That only lasted two weeks. He said he took ill. But as far as he was concerned he'd got his money and that was it."

There was nothing for it: "I had to learn what it was all

about and I ended up physically doing everything which was a good thing because that way I really knew the business inside out. It was hard work. I was pressing, dry-cleaning, driving the van and running the business.''

"Looking back I must have enjoyed it because by the age of 24 I had a thriving businesss.'' It expanded. The attic was converted into a storeroom for more space, another two vans went on the road and he started buying other shops: "From one shop we suddenly had seven or eight shops and two or three vans going out.'' The business was busy and occupied most of his time. It could easily have settled into a useful service to a series of small towns which would potter on making its owner a comfortable, though not extravagant, income for the rest of his days.

Benedetti was not cut out for routine, however attractive it might have been. Nor does his business thinking move along orthodox channels. Having started out his business career with no one there to show him how it 'ought' to be done, he has largely stuck to finding his own solutions. That has often meant perceiving the problems in a different light to his competitors.

"People said to me, 'you don't do it like that'. I turned round and said, 'Well I do and it worked. It's cheaper than the way you do it'.''

Allied to that philosophy was the decline of the traditional dry-cleaning business. He had run his firm for about 10 years, and he had 14 shops. "Then all the crimplenes came out, the drip-dry fabrics, the easily washable stuff. There was less and less work about and competition was tougher. I took a look at what we were doing and thought I had to do something else or expand on a similar theme.''

"It was then that I looked at the garment side of the business and decided to have a go at that.'' He laughs at the scale of the operations he set up: "We put aside ten square feet. That was our garment division.'' It is the same for most innovations. "I was talking to another guy recently and it was the same for him. He started making spectacles at his home, just assembling wee specs in the back garden. Now he employs

106

400. So everyone seems to have started the same way."

He saw a cheap job lot of 1,000 boiler suits advertised, so he bought them: "I rented them to different companies on a '10 here, 20 there' basis and that was really the start of the industrial cleaning side of the business."

This was in 1971 and he was still based in "the same wee place in Kilwinning". "We were doing the ordinary dry-cleaning through the day and boiler suits through the night which wasn't ideal – boiler suits and white dresses don't really mix. But we seemed to manage, and we didn't have enough room to put another machine in anyway."

This was also Benedetti's first real taste of selling. With high street shops there is an element of displaying one's wares and waiting for the custom to arrive. He was now in a different game. To the outsider it may have not have looked much different. Gio Benedetti had just bought in some boiler suits as a little bit of speculation. However, he knew it was very different.

"I'd never really sold anything in my life. This was my first real sales experience. I had no training. I just went and knocked on a few doors. I discovered that I got on well with people and I quite enjoyed it."

He brought his family over from Italy so they could share in his new prosperity. His father ran the presses, his mother worked in one of the dry-cleaning shops. Since his sister was a hairdresser, he bought a hairdressers shop and let it out to her. "I had the whole family operation on the go", he recalls.

It meant he could concentrate on the industrial side. He was good at selling so the contract business grew. The only thing that didn't grow were their premises. It was in an area scheduled for re-development so the council wouldn't give him permission for an extension: "So I ended up putting chicken wire round and wrapping polythene over it to make a lean-to. And we operated underneath this structure. When I think back it was crazy, but we had to do it."

"As long as people get their stuff on time and the quality is there, then how you do it is your business. That is your problem."

2

Then in 1975 the real breakthrough occurred. It turned the Benedetti business from just an ordinary, though unorthodox, dry-cleaning operation into a business which could forge ahead in areas that no one had taken seriously before.

Benedetti was doing some work for the nearby Talbot car plant at Linwood. He had arranged to collect some dry-cleaning and also see the buyer about anything else he could do: "They had 9,000 people working there and I thought 'let's just see what they might want'. So I phoned the buyer up and went to see him. On the way to see him we had to go through the factory floor and I saw all these gloves lying around."

"I didn't say anything at the time. I just went and saw him and said that we cleaned anything." This was the typical Benedetti approach. "It's always been very successful. The only problem comes up when they give you something that's really impossible. Then nothing really is. It may cost us a bit more money but if it is really difficult we can always charge more. You won't have any competition for the work either. The worse it is the better. If nobody else wants to know and you say you can do it, then you've got more business that other companies were not even looking for." So it was with the gloves.

The buyer said there wasn't any business for Benedetti at Linwood: "I said, 'What happens to all those gloves lying around?' He said, 'We just throw them away'. So I said, 'we can clean them'. And he said 'Do you do that?' I said 'Oh yes, all the time'."

" 'How many do you use?' I asked. 'About 15,000 pairs a week', he replied. I knew I couldn't clean 100 pairs but I thought, 'no problem'." Benedetti, sticking to his rule of always trying to appear confident and never let any doubts appear in a customer's mind, said: "Is that all?" and left the buyer's office with a bag of grubby industrial gloves to bring back as a sample of what he could do.

"I hadn't a clue what I was going to do. But I took them back and experimented for a whole week, day and night. We dry-cleaned them, we did this, we did that, we added oil and

108

in the end we made a good job of them. I took them back and the guy was delighted.''

The reconditioned gloves went back onto the shopfloor and no problems arose. The Linwood buyer asked Benedetti if he would be able to cope with the whole order: ''Of course we couldn't, but we knew that if we worked 24 hours a day on them we could make more out of that order than all the other things put together''. They managed.

They had hit on a whole new market which no one else had understood: ''There were a couple of wee companies down south doing it on a piece-meal basis. They were being very selective and just doing the easy bits they wanted to do. Big leather gloves that were easy to do. They weren't touching anything that looked as though it might be a hassle.''

Put very simply, the Benedetti service must have seemed a miracle to anyone in the motor industry trying to cut a few costs. At Linwood the cost of industrial gloves was cut by 50%. By having another company come and recycle the gloves they dramatically cut those costs and incurred no increase in either cost or management time while doing so. They just pay for the clean gloves that come back. Benedetti explains: ''People in that industry just want to build cars. They don't want to bother about gloves and garments. They were going to throw the stuff away anyway and there are no transport costs.''

From initially just cleaning the gloves they moved on to repair work. It increased the number of clean and usable gloves they could return for use, and more importantly, boosted the financial return.

''We started experimenting. We invented patching methods, repairing methods, stitching methods, turning methods and disinfecting methods. At one point even Strathclyde University was involved, because they wanted our report on sterilization.''

Benedetti had made the breakthrough which transformed just another dry-cleaning operation into something special.

From this point on they knew where their biggest market was, they knew they had a winner on their hands.

However, success required growth, and they suffered from the problems of expansion. The problem was compounded because they were effectively transforming the whole nature of their business at the same time. It may once have been fine to manage an ordinary dry-cleaning company by improvising and inventing home-made solutions.

Sticking polythene over a chicken-wire lean-to extension and calling it a new department was no longer the style or the nature of the game. They had an industrial success on their hands. They knew no one had cottoned onto its full potential and they knew their ability to handle all the work they could get their hands on was crucial. More space, and serious space was essential. First there was one Benedetti game that needed to be played out.

His premises were in an area scheduled for redevelopment. "This was handy for me. They said, 'You'll have to move because the road's coming through here and we'll buy you out'. I said 'No, I'm not moving, I love it here'."

In fact, some time earlier, he had bought another building in the nearby seaside town of Ardrossan and rented it out. Fortunately at this point, the people renting it had left. It was a reasonable size, enough to provide at least a stop-gap in the expansion plans. It would allow him to move from a cramped 2,000 square feet to the relative luxury of 6,000 square feet. However, the game with the council continued.

"I still said 'I'm not moving'. I was one of those obnoxious characters who are still saying they're not going to move, even when they've got the bulldozer outside the back door. But I got them up from £30,000 to £50,000 before we finally went. Laundries are not cheap things to build and equip. I needed all the money I could get." When they did move, the transition from lean-to into relatively roomy accommodation was spectacular but short-lived. "It was like a palace compared to what we had been used to. But with expansion it didn't last long."

Growth went at a pace set by Benedetti's efforts to sell his new service: "Linwood was doing well. So they said, 'Why don't you do our plant at Ryton? Talk to them'. So I did.

Other people said, 'Hold on, you're just a wee company. To get that job you'll have to send a van 500 miles there and back, forget it'. I wasn't afraid. We bought a transit and it started going up and down the motorway to Stoke and Dunstable."

"I'd never refuse business, because even with that journey I'd still be making money. The transit had to become a bigger truck and eventually we had an 18 ton truck going up and down the motorways. Then I said as we're already doing Stoke why don't we have a try for the Vauxhall work just up the road."

The Benedetti method of never giving up came into its own: "It wasn't easy. For four years I travelled up and down knocking on their doors. It is that sort of work that people have to come to terms with if they are going to win. Every time I went down south I'd give people a ring and say, 'Right you're coming out for a bit of lunch and a wee chat'. They'd say, 'I haven't any business for you', and I'd say it didn't matter."

"I knew the first time anything happened I was in there. I was really happy. If the other guys announced a price increase I'd say I'd do the work cheaper. And I did. There wasn't much competition but some of it had big names attached. They got some business that way. But it really was wasting a lot of money for the car firms because these other firms were only doing a small amount of the work that could be done. Whereas I could do the lot. What I knew was that once we were into a car factory we could prove how much we could do for them. At the time it was all just theory to them."

Meanwhile the Ardrossan building was not proving large enough: "We had to build another floor, which wasn't ideal with all the heat rising, but it was the best we could do. We had to rent a store just to hold the dirty stuff because we had nowhere else to put it."

Grubby and hand-to-mouth it may have been, but they were making money: "I was making about £100,000 net profit in the Ardrossan days which was around 20% net on turnover. The place was full. I had no overheads. I owned the building. I was paying £1,000 a year in rates and that was it."

His views on how to get the most out of one's work-area are straightforward and obviously heavily influenced by the great discovery of how to maximise production areas with judicious use of chicken-wire and polythene: "Empty space just costs money so the more you can get into one building the better it is. The profit ratio just goes up and then starts to peak because all the overheads are covered. It certainly worked at Ardrossan."

One thing which didn't work at Ardrossan was the look of the business. Sophisticated customers want something a bit more sophisticated from their suppliers. The service may be fine but if it all looks rather hand-to-mouth, then their confidence in one's abilities to maintain the quality required starts to weaken.

"The building in Ardrossan was a sort of old castle in style. It was in fact an old drill hall. I liked it. It was a nice old building but you were getting Vauxhall and Ford saying, 'We must come down and see your place'. I would have to say, 'Well, I don't really know about that', and try to find an excuse. It wasn't really an ideal situation to show anybody."

"It was about par as far as laundries go, but they are by nature dirty, smelly, damp welly-boots type of places. It wasn't any worse than any of our competitors. You walk into most and your first thought is 'God what a mess'."

The other problem this created was, strangely enough, a union one. Not from within his labour-force but from the suspicious work-forces in the car plants. They were being told that in future they would not always be getting new gloves three times a day, but instead would be getting cleaned and recycled ones.

Initial objections were raised: "They were saying 'I am being told to wear gloves that someone else has worn'. They weren't too happy about that, and needed reassurances about hygiene and about what we did to the gloves."

"In the premises in which we were then operating, you couldn't take a union guy along and say, 'This is where the cleaning is done'. The guy would simply have said, 'Fine, thanks very much, there's no way I'm wearing them'. That

112

would have been us out with no business left.''

"So I decided there had to be a new concept here. My idea was to get a nice new modern factory where we could look super-efficient. I thought if we were going to expand we should expand properly. We should get a nice site in a nice area, facing the by-pass so we get free advertising and all the rest of it. It was a big step in my life.''

3

It was also almost the end of the business. They took on the commitment of a huge new factory with all the financing problems that would involve, and as small business luck would have it, ran into the greatest problem they had ever faced at the same time. Half their custom disappeared almost overnight.

They stepped up from being a small private company to the status of a limited company. On 1st May 1980 they became West of Scotland Industrial Clothing Services Limited. The problems of having just the one man running more or less the outfit became apparent: "I was still running a business and at the same time we were having a new factory built at a cost of around £1 million. We had 60,000 square feet built brand-new from scratch."

"I couldn't afford designers or consultants on their 10% fees so I had to do most of it myself. I couldn't get other people to install stuff, so we all just had to work our weekends.''

Even with this sort of stress he still managed to keep tight control of his view of the future. In similar situations, when everything is running ever faster out of control, there is a temptation to keep one's head down and worry simply about immediate problems; to hope that somehow one will survive long enough to reach the easier times when once again one can start to think long-term.

Gio Benedetti managed to avoid this. Even the thinking behind the factory financing was based on a struggle to ensure long-term advantage, rather than easy options to make the short-term viable. He could have simply taken the factory, which was built on an industrial estate in the growth town of

Irvine just down the road, on a rental basis and picked up his first three years rent free.

Instead he chose to buy it: "I'm always looking long-term, so I took another risk and borrowed about £1 million. As a result we will have finished paying for it this year, instead of having to pay £90,000 a year for the next 20 years."

At the time they had nothing like the business to justify the space they were buying. However, Benedetti was convinced and that meant that sooner or later the banks and finance houses would be as well. It was just more selling work for him.

"Getting a grant was a bit of a pantomime", he recalls. But there were grants because they were providing employment for over 100 people. They managed to get £275,000 from the European Economic Community at 10% which, with interest rates at that time ranging between 16% and 18%, was reckoned by Benedetti to be excellent.

Like so many businesses at this stage of development they got help from 3i (Investors in Industry), or ICFC as they were then. They also raised about £100,000 from their old factory. "We got an overdraft of around £200,000 and really everything else we needed we generated from the business. It was all shoestring, but you always seem to have to start with less than you really should."

The then Secretary of State for Scotland, George Younger, opened the new factory on 20 March 1981.

"It was far too big for us when we opened it. There's no doubt about that. Neither did we have the business to justify it. We just took a gamble and bought it. If you run an ordinary business with a few machines in a factory then all you do, if you are adapting or expanding, is unplug them, get a few fork lift trucks in, move them about and off you go. But if you are running a laundry, then you've got to take care of drainage, steam, water-mains and ducting. It becomes a big operation. So when we came here I reckoned it ought to do me for a wee while, despite only filling about a quarter of it. All my calculations were doing all right, the labour was there. Fine, we wouldn't make any money in the first year, but as long as we broke even we would be all right."

114

At this point the work from the Linwood car factory amounted to about half their turnover and was far and away the most profitable part of their business.

Then it was closed down.

"So here we were in this vast factory with overheads ten times what they used to be. Rates were £1,000 a week when we had been used, on the old factory, to paying £1,000 a year. All the rest you can imagine, the heating bills, the borrowing to service the whole enterprise. And I had lost half my business."

"It was", he says with a smile, "a dramatic time in my life".

It was also a challenge to a stubborn man.

"I have never doubted myself. Every time I have achieved something I believe I have achieved it not just because of my personality but because I have confidence in myself. I can do it. Show me it and I'll do it."

"Faced with Linwood closing I thought, 'Right boys, there's no point crying about it, we've got to get the business in'. I knew it was there all the time, I wouldn't have built the factory otherwise. What was against us was the time factor. I needed a bit of time." And time is generally something of which banks are short when they see businesses losing half their potential work and raising their overdrafts at precisely the moment they have moved into what the banks probably considered to be 'grandiose premises'.

The process of convincing the banks there was a future for the company began in earnest: "We had to go to the bank and say, 'Look, we can't give up now'. We were looking for another £50,000 on the overdraft at that time, just to keep us going. I knew we could get the business but I also knew that I couldn't do it overnight."

"So I went to our bankers, The Royal Bank of Scotland, told them that I had this planned and that planned, and could I have the extra facility."

The nightmare, familiar to all small businesses seeking to survive a period of growth and over-stretched resources, began: "I was dealing with the local bank manager and I got a polite letter back from him saying he had to talk to head office about it.''

"They came back and said that not only will we not give you the extra £50,000 but we want your current overdraft reduced by £25,000 within the next few months. They might just as well have said, 'Here's the key to your factory, close its doors now'.''

It was a time for further stubbornness: "As you can imagine, I was very upset at this and I sat down and wrote a stinker of a letter to their head office. I suggested that when they were effectively closing one of their customers down at least they could have the courtesy to come down and see what it was all about and talk to the people concerned. I pointed out that I had always got my business by visiting customers and trying to understand what they wanted. I pointed out I'd been a customer for 20 years and never missed a payment and all of a sudden they want to close me down.''

"The answer to all of that came a week later when we got a guy down saying that they really ought to visit their customers more often. But he still didn't give me the extra £50,000.''

At the same time he received the letter effectively telling him to close down, he had gone along to the Clydesdale Bank and talked to their general manager who was exactly what he needed: "He was quite a character who had very much his own way of doing things.''

Meanwhile the Royal Bank invited Benedetti across to lunch in Edinburgh for an informal chat, and eventually they came up with the money. It was too late: "After my final discussion with the Clydesdale I came out with an extra £100,000 overdraft facility on a shake of hands. I had to tell the Royal I was sorry, but I was moving my business.''

To reinforce the post-Linwood hard-sell efforts he brought in Ed Spence as sales director. Spence had been at school with him but now had good experience in sales and marketing gained in London. With this background behind him he "looked after the shop", coordinating the sales and administrative-related factory operations. This left Benedetti free to fight for, win and consolidate major contracts in England.

"To really make the glove reclamation idea work", Spence recalls, "we needed volume, and I mean volume". The target was most definitely the south, and with that financial recovery.

Benedetti was still finding that the cash crisis was hampering their efforts: "We had the overdraft facility but it wasn't enough. We were juggling it all as much as we could. The Pay-As-You-Earn and the Value Added Tax were all left to the end, we were having to make arrangements to pay them off."

"For an awful six months after Linwood, there really wasn't much happening. Turnover was around £35,000 a month. We were really struggling. Then our sales efforts started to pay off. We got a contract from Ford. Only then we realised we needed new machinery."

"The bank was still helping us, but saying they had gone as far as they would go. There was no money for machinery."

Luckily for West of Scotland, Benedetti had been putting some early earnings into property: "I had always kept it separate from the cleaning business. On the back of that property I borrowed £100,000 and we bought the desperately needed machinery."

Gradually they started making money and started paying off all the arrangements they had made while deep in crisis: "It is important to keep coming up with whatever amount you have promised and that, shit or bust, is precisely what we did. It gives them confidence in you. It also means that after a while you can ask them if you can miss a month and you will be all right."

"When you are in trouble like that, it is all right if you tell people what is going on. I've found through experience that if you don't tell them, you just miss a payment, then they are likely to come along and want the money, end of story."

Gradually the potential of the new space and factory could be built upon: "People could come and see that we were expanding and I was still the cheapest in the glove business." At last they could overcome union doubts in the large motor companies.

"We have had 222 shop stewards from Ford visit our factory. There are sixteen Ford plants and each of them does their own thing, so it is important to let everyone come along. The shop stewards see a nice factory. It's clean, tidy and organised and they can see our machinery producing good gloves."

They also managed to allay other union fears — that recycling would mean job losses elsewhere. "There was no problem selling the concept to the bosses but as far as the workers were concerned we weren't selling anything tangible. So we concentrated on the fact that, as 90% of gloves are imported, we are saving the company and the country money", Benedetti explains. "It's our contribution to the balance of payments if you like, and we're giving 200 people a job."

The work expanded from simply reclaiming gloves to a whole host of other industrial needs. They started work on wipers, polishing bonnets, sleeves, aprons, filter bags, even paper boiler suits: "Basically, anything that is usually thrown away we clean, be it cotton, leather, PVC, rubber, plastic, or whatever." They have stuck to the policy that "most of the stuff we clean no one would touch before".

4

The efforts paid off. Turnover for the year ending in April 1983 had risen to £1,049,977 with pre-tax profits at £31,434. The next year saw turnover improved to £1,759,663 with pre-tax profits racing ahead at £240,282. The directors report noted the 68% increase in turnover and in the language of the accountant remarked "There is now a return to profitability with a substantial, broad customer base throughout the United Kingdom."

Benedetti's beliefs had won: "You cannot do what everyone else is doing. You have to look at it in a different light. If everyone is doing it one way, then maybe it is the best way, but we must always say 'let's look at it another way'."

The individual approach, combined with an insistence that they must look ahead, has resulted in a company which has successfully established a lead in a field which it effectively pioneered. Moreover, the market it has created helps the industry it services. The estimated savings for Ford alone through glove cleaning this year are "well over £1 million" and "over £750,000 for Austin-Rover".

"It is a good sales pitch", says a smiling Benedetti. "All we do is save you money." They are still expanding their service. They now have four people in Ford organising the service full-time. Their own tow-truck goes round the factory. There are 500 glove collecting bins as well as their own store on Ford's premises. They provide their services for "every car plant in Britain," as well as working for British Aerospace, British Steel, Lucas Electrical, Beecham and Burroughs.

By the end of 1985, when they won the Industrial Achievement award, they were processing a weekly total of 300,000 pairs of gloves, 17,000 polishing mops, 12 tons of special lint-free cloth, 4,000 paper boiler suits, 9,000 protective sleeves and aprons and thousands more miscellaneous items.

They still split their workload roughly equally between the glove-led service and the more orthodox industrial dry-cleaning business like roller towels, dust mats, filters and bags.

The market remains highly competitive, but Benedetti still fights them off: "There was a small glove company which was doing some work, and once one of the big boys, Sketchley, had taken a look at the market, they decided to take this company over."

"They said to themselves, 'Why is this wee guy in Scotland doing so well when he's 500 miles away from the main work? We can do it cheaper and better next door, let's get into the business.' "

They did make tentative approaches to see if they could buy Benedetti out but nothing was likely to come of that. So Sketchley had bought the other company.

Benedetti found himself and the salesman from the other company following each other: "He was good but I was better." So Benedetti made him an offer and Tony Hopkins joined up as sales director: "Sketchley bought the business and I bought Tony. In six months we had all their business. Initial were the same. They bought a small company to try and take away some of my business. But they're getting nowhere.''

The official policy is that ''no one is getting in on my patch''. Benedetti will compete as hard as he can, on the basis that eventually the head office will take a look at the glove-cleaning subsidiary that it set up and say: ''We've been in the market for two years and we've got no business. So what's the point? Just leave it all to that wee guy in Scotland.' The big company pulls in its subsidiary and Benedetti has one fewer competitor to worry about.

There is an enormous advantage in being so far ahead in terms of experience and much of that can now be capitalised on. Each cleaning process has taken several years to develop, all the machinery has had to be invented or modified. At the beginning of 1986, for example, they were working on a pneumatically-controlled repairing machine in the hope it would eventually virtually double output from each person. Once that is up and running they hope to be a long way towards developing a laser-operated machine.

They can also manage to lower costs, below any new competitor coming into the market, by a string of energy saving wheezes built up over the years. All the oil extracted from the gloves and wipers is put straight back into the boilers. This amounts to between 700 and 800 gallons each week and saves them an estimated £700 a week on their fuel bill.

''So the more oily things are, the better we like it'', Benedetti comments gleefully. They also sell a lot of cotton from gloves that have to be thrown away and are looking at ways of reconstituting scrapped bits of leather.

To counter the increased energy costs, resulting from its growth in turnover, they have also embarked on an energy-conservation project, which includes a heat and perchloroethylene-recovery system.

They are constantly looking for other areas in which to expand. Benedetti is keeping an eye on the invasion of Scotland by the microchip industry, whose factories require high standards of cleanliness and dust-free materials. He plans to install a special 'factory within a factory' for cleaning garments for the computer industry, where the air will be filtered to produce the required dust-free environment.

In addition they have moved into the fashion area with a service to the large multiple stores stone-washing and bleaching jeans.

5

"From here on it's all going one way", Benedetti declares. Turnover grew 21% on the year to April 1985, standing at £2,131,777 with a pretax profit of £312,944. The sales force was trebled in the year.

The problems with banks are over: "When you're struggling no one wants to know you but now we're doing well everyone wants to come and see us." They are having to utilise every scrap of existing factory space and plan an extension as well. Even office space for the administrative side, which has always been kept to a minimum, is going to be expanded.

A bit of bravado has crept into the way they raise money, fuelled no doubt by the treatment they received when they desperately needed help.

"We needed £500,000 extra overdraft facility. So we said let's go into two or three banks and see what the reaction is. It's been amazing because suddenly they're all desperate for our business. In some ways it's been embarrassing because you've had to refuse and they still keep coming back saying we'd like to make you an offer you can't refuse."

The company is now in the position where it can plan its next steps. The Unlisted Securities Market has become the traditional move at this point and Benedetti agrees: "When we reach the £1 million profit mark, which hopefully we should do within the next couple of years, we would like to go onto the USM. We are planning ahead for it. We would be the first in our industry to do it and we would go on with a multiple of around 15."

Benedetti doesn't deny there is a bit of status involved in the idea of a listing but, sticking to the old principles, he would like the chance of raising money more easily. "Assuming it would put a couple of million into the company, that would enable us to clear our overdraft for example. At the moment we're paying £100,000 a year for that. We'd be rid of that expense and it would give us the money we need for expansion.''

In Benedetti's view the business is there; the amount they pick up is limited only by the resources they have available for expansion. The USM, to a company in this position, would seem to be the only answer.

It would also provide the finance to allow a company with a dominant market share to go for other related markets. To a great extent West of Scotland, or Industrial Clothing services as it now calls itself, now dominates the glove market; expansion of its share will mean sweeping up small pockets of work which it has ignored in the past as it went for the major sources of work.

They plan to continue to use their own particular management style to grow parts of the market other companies have either not noticed, or ignored because of the perceived profitability.

Benedetti is keener than ever to capitalise on his company's strength and expertise. Reviewing how other major companies run has made him more aware of his company's strengths: ''We've always tried to keep our eye on the future. For example, back in the Ardrossan days between 10 and 15 years ago, we had a computer. Now we have a big System 36 one which runs 70 screens. It's bigger than we need but I've always planned on the grounds we're only going one way. Think or buy small and whatever it is will be out of date a year later and cost you twice as much to replace.''

''Recently I was looking at a new contract which would be worth about £3 million over the next three years. At the moment it's done by a big company and I went down to have a look at how they were doing it.'' He lapses into the language of a Scottish schoolboy to describe the operation and to express his amazement at how backward they were. ''They were using jotters throughout'', he said. ''Somebody was having to write down a note of everything that came through. We've been completely computerised for five years now.''

122

The factory now thrives. A new flooring is going down to continue the efforts to take the laundry business out of the "welly boots" world and it is packed with pallets of very, very clean gloves. Over a weekend they have about 600,000 pairs on site. The growing workforce are relatively happy, given the nature of the work, and the policy is to pay above the going local rate. It is not a unionised workforce but a system of works committees, with regular and formal meetings, provides them with a voice in the way the factory is run.

Benedetti now has an efficient management team in place and though he is obviously less-involved than he was he is still, undoubtedly, the dominant personality and force in the company. He owns 80%, his father has a 10% stake and 3i owns the remaining 10% chunk.

There is no doubt in Benedetti's mind as to why his company has been successful: "I would say that much of it is due to aggression. Not real aggression but something in my nature. I'm a reasonable guy. If someone's telling me something I'll listen but I am forceful to a certain degree. Things get done. Things get moving."

He also feels that being the top man one has to be flamboyant. "I drive a Lotus. I drive a Jag. I get a lot of publicity and I direct that to good advantage. People want to deal with people who are known. I get people phoning me up and saying, 'I was talking to Joe Bloggs, a good friend of yours', and I've never met the guy."

"In that respect I use the publicity for the business. It creates business."

He doesn't feel that there is anything unique about his style or his personality, although he does stress the need for common sense to underpin people's decision-making processes in business. He now sees things from the other side of the fence as well. He is a director of ASSET, the Ardrossan and Saltcoats Enterprise Trust, which provides local help for small businesses and so aims to create jobs.

"We have £500,000 of EEC money to lend and I am doing the banker's side of the business for once. We can lend up to £10,000 to help an idea along. But we get engineers in with very good ideas who just don't want to go out and sell. And vice versa. We get guys in who are salesmen but who have got nothing behind them. Without substance you can sell for a while but eventually you get found out.''

He feels the ability to sell is the most important asset: ''Unless you can sell you're nothing. You can have a great product but if you haven't sold it, what's the point?''

The other strength required is financial planning. When he started out he simply went along to an accountant and got help putting together a basic financial plan. He believes the important thing is that the person in command of the business understands that inside out. There is little point in having professionally prepared plans if one does not know what they mean in every detail.

At ASSET people have to bring in their projections for their business. ''You ask them questions and they say, 'well my accountant told me that'. You have to reply, 'Come on, you're the main man, the accountant's only your advisor, what does this figure mean? Why are you going to spend that?' They finish up replying that they don't really know.'' In the old days he admits, he probably did the same initially. The desire to be in total control of the business as it started to grow forced the habit out of him.

Benedetti also stresses the importance of being confident and of relying completely on your products being better than anyone else's. Again he cites recent experiences assessing businesses for ASSET. ''You find people trying to move into markets they know nothing about and relying on what they've read in a book.''

''We had one guy in who was going to start up making concrete statues and blocks and spend about £50,000 starting up the business. But he knew nothing about concrete. He said he could learn, but what of the people in the market who have got ten years advantage of expertise on him? The new guy is going to make all the mistakes and the old hand is going to eat him up for breakfast.''

The same argument could easily be applied to the youthful Benedetti starting off his career in dry-cleaning. That is where the personality comes into play. Stubborn and aggressive people tend not to mind the competition and they will probably find a way of winning through.

Gio Benedetti now lives well. His sales director, Ed Spence, remembers him at school as being a character apart, not just because he was the immigrant but because of the resources of energy within him waiting for an outlet. However, even he could not have foreseen the way it would work out.

Benedetti now has a big house with three acres of grounds overlooking the sea at West Kilbride. He has a tennis court. He is building a swimming pool. He has a holiday house on the Isle of Arran on the other side of the Firth. He water-skis there. Now he has a two and a half year old daughter. "Another jewel in my life", he says.

On the surface, his resolve and energy on behalf of the company might now be expected to slacken. But like all the winners he is the type of person whose life is completely bound up with his creation, his company and its success.

His stubbornness is deep within him and unlikely to disappear. In his early days he used to swim the 11 miles across the sea from Largs to Millport and back again on a Sunday. This came out in conversation when he was trying, after failure to convince a bank, to borrow £2,000 from a merchant banker. "He lent it to me because he thought 'well this guy must be worth a couple of thousand. He has to be a stayer if he can swim 11 miles in the bloody sea just as a hobby'."

HOW TO BECOME WINNERS OF THE FUTURE

All the five winners I have looked at in this book are very different people running very different businesses. That is very much the joy of the Industrial Achievement Award.

In the early days of judging the award there were often worries that it would finish up honouring only the hi-tech successes. For a time there was a belief that the only companies which would be long-term successes were those being run in the university towns by small teams of boffins. From these, it was argued, would come both the future of industry and the future for employment.

Like many business beliefs, it was founded on the erroneous assumption that something that looked new must be better than something which just looks like another business.

As far as the award is concerned, the emergence of Norfrost, Denford and Industrial Cleaning Services shows that what might seem ordinary businesses can get off the ground and grow just as well as any computer-related business.

As for the boffins myth, probably the most significant point about all the winners in this book is that none of them went to university or business school.

Common to them all is the notion of starting a business from within their own experience and never losing sight of their basic objective.

It is too easy to be seduced by the purveyors of management theory. Many a simple business idea has been over-complicated because its instigator feels that something simple is going to be seen as hopelessly unsophisticated by their peers.

As this book has shown, this is not true, all the winners have survived because they refused to believe people who told them that they would fail. As Pat Grant of Norfrost said: 'If you're running a race, you can't have people stopping you halfway'.

That is not a call for people to be pig-headed. It does mean that people who refuse to be over-awed by theory are the ones who will succeed.

All of the winners had such a solid belief in what their experience had taught them that they survived the first hurdle of discouragement. Moreover, they had grounded themselves so deeply in that experience they were able to ensure that, from the beginning, the business was something which could work.

There are lessons to be learned from all of the winners in this book and, keeping those lessons firmly in mind, there is no reason why many others should not follow in their path.

YOUR EXPERIENCE IS YOUR GREATEST ASSET: MAKE IT WORK FOR YOU

All experience is important. You must make sure that it works for you. From the smallest beginnings, like the young Alex Grant taking a motor scooter to bits, to the long career in electronics that Tony Martinez turned to his advantage, you will find that you have accumulated expertise and knowledge along the way. In your own business all this can be used.

Crucially you should look for a gap in the market which your experience, great or small, enables you to fill. When doing this, and indeed through all your efforts running a business, you should always try to think long-term.

As the early days of Microvitec showed, thinking long-term can be the hardest part. It will be all too easy to fight the daily fires and never have the time or, harder still, the energy to think ahead. But it must be done. Not only do you lose direction without long-term thought, but it enables other competitors or disgruntled providers of your finance to bring your efforts to an untimely end.

You should reinforce your experience in the most positive ways available. And you should make sure that you use it effectively.

Think along the lines of what Alex Grant called the 'Japanese trick'. See how others do something and then take the best ideas and adapt them to the business that you are developing.

Follow the example of Tony Martinez and carry a notebook at all times. When an idea strikes you, note it down. Never imagine that a good idea will return and that you will remember it later on. You will be far too busy for that.

Keep a close watch on your competitors, not because you want to do what they are doing, but so that you can do what they are not doing. Gio Benedetti won through not just by having a bright idea, but also through deciding that he would do work that his competitors thought was not worth doing.

PREPARE YOURSELF TO FIGHT THROUGH THE DISCOURAGEMENT AHEAD

Pat Grant made it clear that the most important point was to make sure that no one could stop you when you were halfway through your task. It is vital to recognise from the start that people on all sides will make discouraging noises just when you are having a few doubts yourself. At that point strengthen your resolve.

Ignore , as the Grants and everyone else in this book did, the advice of wiser counsels when they tell you that the business will not work. Step up your efforts, as Gerald Denford did, and make sure that no one is going to beat you for lack of stamina and long, determined hours.

Take the opportunity of explaining the basis for your confidence to your providers of funds. As several of our winners have found, an enthusiastic explanation to the bank just as you hit another crisis can pay off handsomely.

Follow the advice of the Battersbys and refuse to get yourself into the position where you feel that accountants are panicking you into what you see as negative decisions. Back your own entrepreneurial and commercial judgements.

KEEP BUSINESS PLANS AND DEALINGS WITH ADVISORS SIMPLE AND EFFECTIVE

Try to ensure from the start that your accountants, solicitors and bankers are going to be effective. Too many businesses start off with advisors who are not backing them whole-heartedly. Advisors have to be utterly convinced of what you are doing before they will provide the extra backing that you need.

Remember the importance of the business plan. It is no good having a fancy financial plan if you do not understand it inside out yourself. Remember the advice from Gio Benedetti based on his experience of advising fledgling businesses. There is little point in having professionally prepared plans if you do not know what they mean in every detail. The answer, as Benedetti made plain, was 'Come on, you're the main man, the accountant's only your advisor, what does this figure mean? Why are you going to spend that?'

Keep your dealings with banks and accountants simple and straightforward. And, as far as is possible, honest. There will be times when you will have to make your story as attractive as possible to ensure that your lines of credit stay intact. Do that, but never mislead your advisors completely. If they find out, and they are likely to do so, they will never trust you again.

Raising funds is the next step on from sorting out advisors and getting business plans agreed. All the winners in this book found that the initial help from 3i for funding was crucial. It is another example of the great work that 3i, in its various guises and names, has been doing for so many years.

The other maxim which could be drawn from the early days of all our winners is that having financial partners at the beginning is something to be avoided. As the idea of the business gets off the ground there will always be close friends or colleagues who discuss the idea with you and who seem willing and eager to make it work.

But ideas are unique. Two people may have similar objectives. The ways that the objectives can be attained will differ. If a partner is needed because it is another method of funding then, on the experience of the winners in this book, the projected partnership should be dropped as swiftly as possible. If the partner is going to be there to provide expertise rather than cash, keep him or her.

All the winners found dreadful problems with Government agencies over grants or related political adventures. The answer is probably not to look upon grants or any Government help as being an essential. They all depend on a vast connection of political interests which, if examined, make no sense at all to the aspiring entrepreneur.

The lesson here would be that if something is available and it looks as though it will be fairly simple to achieve, then an effort should be made. If it looks difficult, then it should be left. At that point in the business's history there will be much more important areas in which to concentrate time and effort.

Later in your business's development you will be tempted to go for a listing, either straight to the stock market or via the un-listed securities market. When you are thinking along those lines, pause, take a deep breath, and then read again the section of the case study on Microvitec which deals with their USM debut.

Make sure in your own mind that you are convinced that you understand the sheer scale of the effort required. And, even more important, that you can heed the warnings of Tony Martinez: 'I think that if you repeated it over and over again 20 times it would not go amiss. Remember young companies have small organisational structures with all their directors as operational directors. If you are already working 70 hours a week, and you decide to go public, where do you get the time from? You have to take all your directors and spend a tremen-dous amount of time with solicitors, accountants, merchant bankers and brokers. It is an extremely time-consuming affair'.

LOCATE YOUR BUSINESS WHERE YOU WANT IT TO BE

The location of the business is crucial. All of the winners picked an area where they thought they could run their business best. This goes against the generally held belief that businesses should be started in areas where the advantages of regional aid or industrial estates are available.

It makes sense, Microvitec could have been sited in a Welsh valley. There was no geographical need to be in Bradford. Norfrost would have a much easier distribution network if it had been sited just outside of Manchester.

But that would have ignored the importance of experience and expertise within those businesses. Neither of them could have won through anywhere but in their present locations. And if that seems daft to the experts in locating industries, then they should look at the results.

MAKE THE MOST OF YOUR STRENGTHS AS INDIVIDUALS

A small business has the advantage over large businesses in terms of its human scale. You must make the most of this. As Pat Grant made plain, your products must be designed from the customer's point of view, and the way that you sell them must be individually targeted. The Battersby's success story in initially writing personal letters to hundreds of potential customers shows how the advantage of being a small business can be brought into play. Pat Grant's efforts with the various electricity boards hammers the point home.

Make sure that your customers know the extent to which you can provide an advantage through your size and flexibility. The Battersby's policy of keeping offcuts of cable for future use on specific jobs is a good example. Learn the language of your prospective customers and investors and learn to communicate with them as individuals.

Remember the advantages of confidence. Pat Grant got a

good price from the Japanese because she was confident in what she knew and what she wanted.

Follow the Grant's example wherever possible. Manufacture as many components as you can yourself. Don't pay other people's overheads. Make sure that flexibility extends to keeping your business efficient. Basic practices like saving energy, cutting back on waste and using all the space you have are much easier to implement as a small and growing business than they are for an established and cumbersome company. Exploit this advantage that you have over your larger competitors.

BUILD THOSE INDIVIDUAL STRENGTHS INTO THE ORGANISATION

When a small business starts out in life it has the best possible structure. It is a tight-knit team of highly motivated individuals with a clearly defined objective and an understanding of the specific tasks required.

The trick is to ensure that as the business grows those skills of allying the individual with the organisation can be retained.

Of the winners in this book Microvitec has moved the farthest in terms of growth and size, and Tony Martinez's views on how to translate the small team through what he called 'the workshop stage' into a fully fledged corporate structure are the most valuable.

You must make people feel that they are part of a team, and that company growth and personal growth are inextricably intertwined. A system which allows all employees to formally participate in the company is vital. It is important to establish a communications system which is part of the structure. We can all make ourselves believe that an *ad hoc* communications system is adequate. The problem is that at times of crisis when you need greater and faster communication within your business than ever before, the *ad hoc* system will tend to collapse. By establishing a formal structure you can avoid this.

You need a good balance of skills across your team. The

lessons from the winners in this book is that manufacturing, marketing, selling and financial skills are the areas needed. But rarely have any of them got the balance right. In particular they all underestimated the importance of good financial controls.

And, crucially, they all underestimated the importance of having effective management information systems in place. Again this is an area where weaknesses only really become apparent when you hit a crisis. And being stuck in a crisis with unreliable information on how you are doing and whether you can reach your targets is disastrous.

The planning process as you set about expansion should be documented, logical and should be the result of formally presenting ideas and having the ideas of others in the company bounced off them. The point about this, as Tony Martinez pointed out, is that the methodology creates a discipline in your planning and organisation pocedures.

WINNERS OF THE FUTURE

When Norman Tebbitt made the presentation of the 1983 award he said: 'Our hope must be that some of our small firms will grow into big ones, that somewhere a new Rolls is meeting a new Royce, a new Marks is meeting a new Spencer and discussing how their business might grow'.

It is often hard when looking at small business to see how they could ever become a truly large concern. There is a tendency to look at a small factory producing freezers, or an industrial laundry business, or a husband and wife team providing electronic connectors, and say that it is all very well as it is but there are limitations to its eventual growth.

What should be remembered is that the business observer of the time, had he looked at the market stall that was the beginning of the Marks and Spencer empire, would probably have said the same thing.

And they would have said it for the same reason. Business observers nearly always look at the wrong things. They look at the conveyor belt and try to work out the possible growth of the market it supplies. Or they look at a marketing strategy or foreign competition.

In short they look at the business in isolation and fail to concentrate properly on the people who have created that business.

This book has tried to rectify that, and tried to dispose of business myths along the way. The image of the business person as someone remote from ordinary experience stems from looking too hard at theory, and not simply trying to understand people as people.

There are many people with similar qualities to the winners in this book. They must try and remove the obstacles the business theorists put in their way. If this book proves anything, it is that the important qualities are experience, good sense, determination and a desire to feel the satisfaction of a good job done.